This book belongs to:

DAD'S BO

OLD-FASHIONED FUN FOR THE FAMILY

PaRragon

Bath · New York · Singapore · Hong Kong · Cologne · Delhi · Melbourne

OK

This is a Parragon Publishing Book
This edition published in 2008

Parragon Publishing
Queen Street House
4 Queen Street
Bath BA1 1HE, UK

Designers: Timothy Shaner and Christopher Measom
Project Director: Alice Wong
Project Assistants: Jacinta O'Halloran, Betsy Davis, Nicholas Liu
Art Assistant: Joanne Berei

Fairy Tales retold by Wendy Wax
Music arrangement by Frank Zuback
Recipes by Lena Tabori

Printed in Thailand.

10 9 8 7 6 5 4 3 2 1

Contents

Contents

If the new American father feels
bewildered and even defeated, let
him take comfort from the fact that

whatever he does in any fathering situation he has a fifty percent chance of being right.

—Bill Cosby

The Gingerbread Boy

Once upon a time there were a little old woman and a little old man who lived in a little old house. The little old man could often be found dozing in his chair (making little old snores) while the little old lady brewed tea in a little old kettle and made meals in a little old pan.

One morning, the little old woman and the little old man received a telegram saying their grandson was coming to visit.

"I know!" said the little old woman. "I'll bake a gingerbread boy for him."

The little old woman mixed the gingerbread batter, shaped it into a boy, and slid it into the oven, leaving the door slightly open by mistake.

"I must go to the market," the little old woman said to the little old man. "Take the gingerbread boy out in ten minutes."

"Yes, dear," said the little old man. But five minutes later, he was fast asleep.

"Hey!" shouted gingerbread boy, who was getting really hot. He peered out of the oven but the little old woman who had made

The Gingerbread Boy

him was nowhere in sight, and the little old man was snoring loudly. The gingerbread boy climbed out onto the stove between the little old kettle and the little old pan and looked around. "It's boring here," he said. He raced out the door, and ran and ran until he reached a group of children playing in a field. The children saw him and licked their lips.

"*Yum!*" said a girl. But before she could break off an arm, the gingerbread boy ran away, calling:

"I am a little gingerbread boy. I have run away from a little old woman and a little old man, a little old kettle and a little old pan, and I can run away from you, I can, I can." And so he ran and ran and came to an old brown cow drooling with hunger.

"*Moo!*" went the cow. But before he could nip off an ear, the gingerbread boy ran away, calling:

"I am a little gingerbread boy. I have run away from a little old woman and a little old man, a little old kettle and a little old pan, a field full of children, and I can run away from you, I can, I can." And so he ran and ran and came to a sly fox.

"I am a little gingerbread boy," he said to the fox. "I have run away from a little old woman and a little old man, a little old

The Gingerbread Boy

kettle and a little old pan, a field full of children and an old brown cow, and I can run away from you, I can, I can." But as he ran, so did the fox—and foxes are fast! Soon they came to a wide river.

"Would you like to go across?" the fox asked, jumping into the water.

"Sure," said the gingerbread boy, catching his breath.

"Climb on my tail," the fox suggested.

The gingerbread boy did just that. But as the water got deeper, the tail got wetter.

"You'll stay dryer if you climb on my back," the fox suggested.

The gingerbread boy climbed on the fox's back. Soon the water deepened.

"You'd better climb on my nose," the fox suggested.

So the gingerbread boy climbed on the fox's nose—which was a *big* mistake. For the fox opened his mouth, and gobbled the gingerbread boy up!

"Delicious," said the fox, satisfied. "Gingerbread boys are meant to be eaten, not to be out running around." And he curled up under a tree, drifted off into a nap, and dreamt about more scrumptious gingerbread boys.

Is That a Box?

Never throw away a cardboard box! The imaginary play a child can have with a box is endless. Use brown paper to cover up boxes that have markings. Then, with a few cuts and some new marks, your child can be master of his or her own house, a racecar driver, or a chef. The instructions below are just a start—think boat, sled, castle, television set, refrigerator, puppet theater. . . .

cardboard boxes, masking tape, scissors, markers, glue

PLAYHOUSE

1. Tape and secure together the flaps of a large appliance box.
2. Draw door and windows on the sides of the box and cut along their outlines, leaving hinges of cardboard so that they can open and close.
3. Have your child help decorate by drawing bricks, curtains, or window boxes on the outside.

RACECAR

1. You will need a box large enough for a child to sit in. Cut away the flaps and cut down the top of the box to the chest level of your sitting child.
2. From the extra cardboard, cut out a steering wheel for your child to hold. You can also cut out a play key.
3. Cut out four wheels from the extra cardboard for your child to glue on.
4. Make an L-shaped cut in one side of the box to make a door, folding back the flap to create a hinge-like effect.
5. Draw a dashboard on the inside of the box, complete with speedometer and gauges. Red buttons for "eject" and "maximum speed" are fun additions.
6. Don't forget the outside of the car! Add headlights and fenders; decorate with sponsor logos, numbers, and favorite shapes.

KITCHEN STOVE

1. Set a large box whichever way the height best suits your child, but make sure there is a flat surface on top.
2. Draw on circles for burners and knobs.
3. Cut an oven door into the front.

Pop! Goes the Weasel!

A Pancake of Your Own

Use a spoon (or chicken baster) to dribble your child's initial—backwards—onto the pan a few seconds before you spoon on the circle of pancake batter. When you flip the pancake, the initial will appear on the other side. You can also make animal outlines, dollar signs, or heart shapes using this method. A good pancake pan is a great help. This recipe is from three great dads: Philip, Rob, and Franco.

1 1/2 cups unbleached white flour (or corn meal)
1 tablespoon sugar
1/4 tablespoon salt
1 tablespoon baking powder
3 eggs, separated
1/4 cup melted butter (easily done in the microwave)
2 cups milk

1. Preheat oven to 200°F and put a plate in to warm.
2. In a large bowl, combine dry ingredients.
3. In another bowl, beat egg yolks with the melted butter and milk. Stir into the flour mixture.
4. Beat egg whites until they are fluffy and fold them into the batter.
5. Heat a lightly buttered frying pan over medium-high heat.
6. Dribble your initial or shape onto the pan first. Then drop a large spoonful of batter on top of the browning initial. When the bubbles start to dry, flip and brown on the other side.
7. Keep pancakes warm in the oven until ready to serve.
8. Serve with your favorite toppings— applesauce, maple syrup, lemon juice and powdered sugar, or your favorite jam. (If you are a Swede, it has to be lingonberries; if you are Hungarian, apricot jam will be your choice).

Serves 4 to 6

Trust me, you can't go wrong with eggs, and there are endless variations. Great scrambled eggs are a must, and egg-soaked bread—french toast—is divine. And then there are One-Eyed Sailors. Philip Patrick, father of the charming Eleanor, told me about his dad making them while his mom slept in. Then Franco (my guy) said, "No, no, no. That's an Egg in a Nest, and Jay (his son) had it for breakfast with maple syrup when he was a little guy." So, whatever you call it, it's a big hit.

Great Scrambled Eggs

4 eggs
1/4 cup milk
1/2 cup diced tomatoes
1/4 cup grated cheddar or Swiss cheese
salt and pepper to taste
1 tablespoon butter

1. Break eggs into a bowl and add milk. Beat with a fork until the eggs are frothy, then add tomatoes, cheese, and salt and pepper.

2. Melt the butter in a nonstick frying pan. When it sizzles, lower the heat, pour in the egg mixture, and move it around with the back of the fork. Cook until the egg forms soft curds and serve immediately.

Serves 2

Other tasty additions to scrambled eggs: small pieces of ham or bacon; sauteed and chopped zucchini, peppers, mushrooms, or onions; mozzarella, havarti, or cottage cheese; chopped parsley, oregano, basil, thyme, or chives.

Eggs are the Best

French Toast

6 eggs
1/2 cup milk
dash cinnamon or nutmeg, or 1/2
* teaspoon vanilla extract (optional)*
12 thick slices challah or your
* favorite softer-type bread*
4 tablespoons butter

1. Put warming plate in a 250°F oven.
2. In a wide bowl, whisk together eggs, milk, and optional seasoning.
3. Soak both sides of the bread until completely soaked.
4. Heat a large frying pan over high heat for 20 seconds and then reduce heat to medium. Add the butter.
5. When the butter stops sizzling, add pieces of soaked bread. Cook until golden brown, about 3 to 4 minutes on each side.
6. Keep warm in the oven and serve immediately when the rest of the toast is done. Serve with applesauce, syrup, or powdered sugar and cinnamon.

Serves 6

One-Eyed Sailors

4 slices challah, rye, or another
* favorite bread*
4 tablespoons butter
4 eggs

1. Use the rim of a glass to press and cut a circle out of the middle of each slice of bread. (You can save the circles to make French Toast).
2. In a non-stick frying pan, heat the butter over low heat until it is melted and the pan is hot.
3. Put slices of bread in the pan.
4. Crack eggs, one at a time, into a small bowl and slide each egg into the hole in each slice of bread.
5. Cook for a few minutes until the white of the egg is firm. Then flip and cook for a couple of minutes on the other side until the yolk is as firm as you like.
6. Serve with maple syrup.

Serves 2

Food

What do you get when you put three ducks in a box?

A box of quackers.

What kinds of crackers do firemen like in their soup?

Firecrackers.

What starts with "t," ends with "t," and is filled with "t"?

A teapot.

What do you call a train loaded with bubble gum?

A chew-chew train.

Why did the boy throw butter out the window?

He wanted to see a butterfly.

Why is a cook mean?

Because he beats eggs, mashes potatoes, and whips cream.

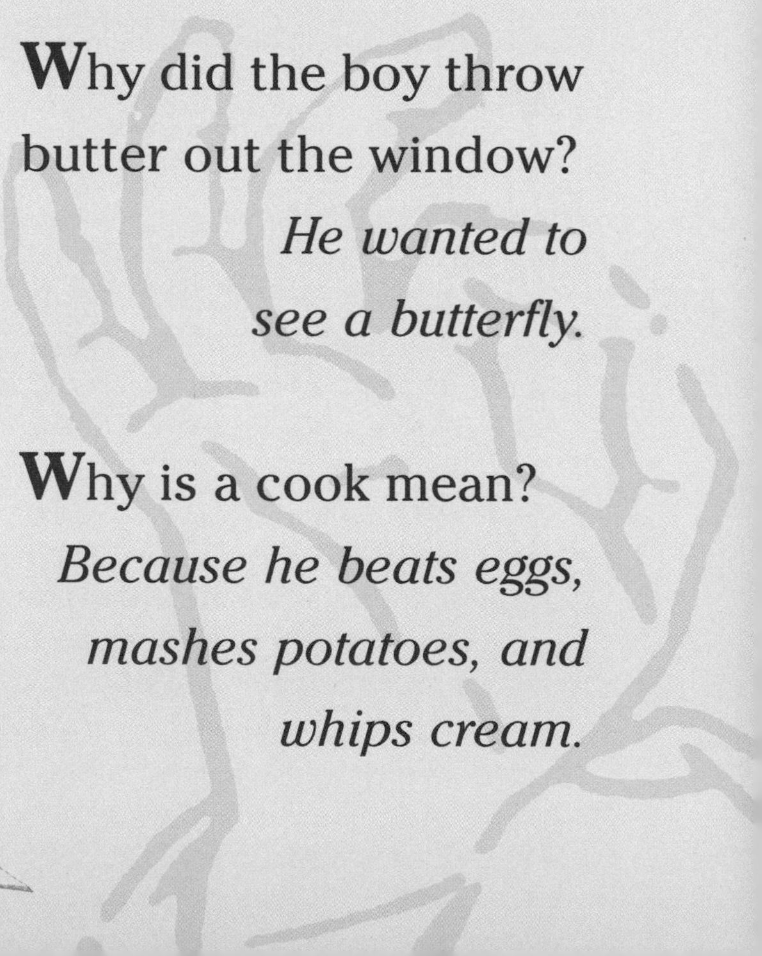

What did the baby corn
say to the mama corn?
I want my pop corn!

What do you
call tired popcorn?
Pooped corn.

What do you call a
peanut in outer space?
An astronut.

What happens when
you tell an egg a joke?
It cracks up!

How do you make a
milkshake?
Say BOO! to a cow.

Why did the cow
eat a chocolate bar?
*Because he wanted to
make chocolate milk.*

Why did the cookie
go to the doctor?
Because he felt crummy.

What do you call a dog
on fire?
A hot dog.

Jokes

Betty Botter bo

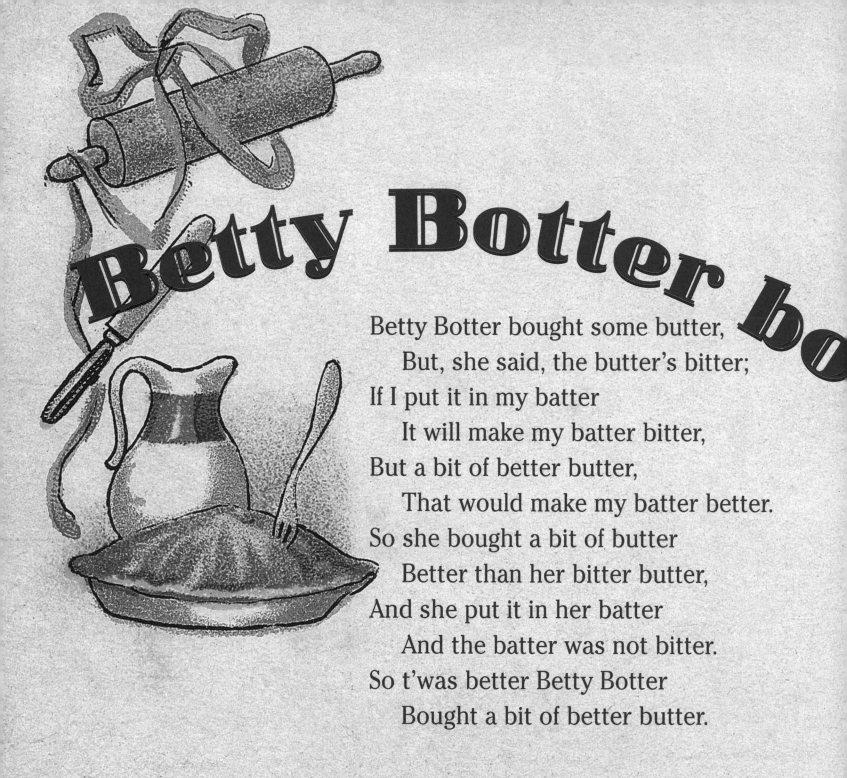

Betty Botter bought some butter,
But, she said, the butter's bitter;
If I put it in my batter
It will make my batter bitter,
But a bit of better butter,
That would make my batter better.
So she bought a bit of butter
Better than her bitter butter,
And she put it in her batter
And the batter was not bitter.
So t'was better Betty Botter
Bought a bit of better butter.

The Pied Piper of Hamelin

Once upon a time the village of Hamelin sat upon the banks of a great river. The people who lived there considered themselves lucky, for they were all rich, ate the finest foods, wore the most stylish clothes, and lived in the most elegant houses. But even so, Hamelin had a big problem: rats—mean, gray rats with sharp, gray teeth everywhere you looked. These rats were very smart, and they never walked into the traps or ate the poison the villagers set out for them. Instead, they nibbled on food, clothing, and even toes! Determined to find a solution, the people of Hamelin went straight to the mayor.

"LET'S GET CATS TO KILL THE RATS!" the mayor proposed.

Everyone cheered, proud that they had elected such a firm and smart man.

Within a week, everyone in town had at least three cats. (They never bought just one of anything.)

For two weeks, the mayor's plan worked splendidly. The cats ate the rats, and the people of Hamelin forgot their worries. But then something strange happened. The cats started dying and the

The Pied Piper of Hamelin

rats started multiplying. Soon, there were more rats than ever—everywhere you looked! A meeting was called in the Town Hall.

"We've tried poison and traps," said a woman.

"And thousands of cats," said a man.

"How can we get rid of the rats?" the people cried out.

The mayor shrugged helplessly.

Suddenly, there was a knock at the door. When the mayor's assistant opened it, a tall, thin stranger dressed in brightly colored silks entered the room. A long feather stuck out of his purple hat, and he carried a beautiful, golden pipe.

"I am the Pied Piper," the stranger said, "and I've freed other villages of beetles and bats. Pay me a thousand gold coins, and I'll get rid of all your rats!"

"We'll give you *fifty* thousand gold coins if you succeed!" said the mayor.

"Very well," said the Pied Piper. "By daybreak tomorrow, there won't be a rat left in Hamelin!" Then he was gone.

That evening at sunset, the magical tones of a pipe wafted through the village of Hamelin. Rats scampered out of every nook and cranny in every house, shop, and office, to flock at the heels of the Pied Piper. When he reached the river, the Pied Piper continued to play as he waded straight in. By the time the water reached his chest, all the rats had drowned and every last one of them was swept away by the current.

"I'd like my fifty thousand gold coins," the Pied Piper told the mayor the next morning.

"Fifty thousand!" exclaimed the greedy mayor, for, though the village had money, it was needed to maintain the fancy gardens, parks, and museums. Now that the rats were gone, why pay the piper what he had promised, he reasoned; the town's problem had already been solved.

"Then give me a thousand gold coins, as I originally requested!" said the Piper, annoyed.

"I'll give you fifty," said the mayor, "which I think is very generous indeed."

The townspeople agreed, for they loved their gardens, parks, and museums. "You should simply be grateful for what you get," they said.

"You can keep your fifty measly gold coins!" cried the Piper. "You broke your promise, and you'll soon regret it." Then he disappeared.

That night, the people of Hamelin slept soundly, for they no longer worried about rats crawling into bed with them. When the sound of the Pied Piper's pipe wafted through the streets, only

The Pied Piper of Hamelin

the children heard it. In their pajamas, the children of Hamelin—from toddlers to teenagers—left their houses and followed the Pied Piper to a dark forest at the edge of town, mesmerized by the magical tones of his pipe.

The Pied Piper led the procession through the forest to the foot of a majestic mountain. He played three mysterious notes, and a giant piece of the mountain creaked open like a door. In he marched, playing his golden pipe, with the children at his heels. When they were all inside, the mountain closed up behind them.

"Wait for me!" cried a boy with a twisted ankle, who hadn't been quick enough. But the door was nowhere to be found.

When the sun came up, the boy returned to the village of Hamelin, where everyone was looking for their children—including the mayor, whose eight sons and eight daughters had all disappeared during the night.

The boy with the twisted ankle told everyone what had happened. The mayor and the townspeople wailed and cried for their children, but it was no use.

The Pied Piper and the children of Hamelin were never seen again, and, to this day, no one has ever found an entrance to the mountain.

Five Toes

This little pig went to market;

This little pig stayed at home;

This little pig had roast beef;

This little pig had none;

This little pig said, "Wee, wee!

I can't find my way home."

Knee Rides

Knee rides are one of the first games children adore. You can bounce older babies gently on knees to elicit great belly laughs. Give older children a real "wild" ride on your foot, holding onto their hands.

This is the way the ladies ride,
Tripity trot, tripity trot
On their way to town.
(bounce child gently on knee)

This is the way the gentlemen ride,
Gallop-a-gallop, gallop-a-gallop
On their way to town.
(bounce faster)

This is the way the farmers ride!
Clompity-clomp, clomp, clomp!
On their way to town.
(bounce really fast)

Ride a cock-horse to Branbury Cross,
  To buy little Johnny a galloping horse;
It trots behind and it ambles before,
  And Johnny shall ride till he can ride no more.

Trot, trot to Boston town
  to get a stick of candy.
One for you, and one for me,
  and one for Dicky Dandy.

The Ant and the Cricket

Once upon a hot summer, on the tip of a leafy branch, lounged a cricket. All day and all night, she sang cheerful songs while watching a long line of ants slave away on the ground below.

"Hey, down there!" she called between songs. "How can you work in this heat?"

"We're . . . storing . . . food . . . for . . . the . . . winter," answered an ant, struggling under the weight of a piece of grain.

"But winter is months away!" shouted the cricket. "You've got to learn to relax."

"We can't," explained another ant from beneath a morsel of sugar. "It takes us all summer to fill our winter pantry. And we'll only make it through the winter if our pantry is full."

The cricket shrugged. "As I always say, summer is for singing, winter is for worrying," she said, nibbling a bright green leaf. "Take a break, and I'll teach you a song."

"Thanks, but no thanks," said an ant, rolling a bread crumb in front of him.

The Ant and the Cricket

All summer long, the cricket sang while the ants worked. Soon autumn came and the leaves fell from the trees. The cricket climbed down from the bare tree. She was too hungry and tired to sing more than a line or two of a song.

"Brrr," she said, making her way through crunching leaves. "It's getting chilly." She wished the ants were still around—not that they'd been great company, but at least she could talk to them.

Soon an early frost covered the fields, and the cricket felt hungrier than ever. She fed on the few dry stalks left on the frozen ground, but that barely gave her enough strength to move. Her throat was so dry she couldn't sing a single note.

Then it began to snow. Trembling and famished, the cricket curled up under a tree, closed her eyes, and dreamed of the carefree summer days. She awoke to the faint sound of singing. It was coming from a speck of light in the distance. Gathering all her strength, she made her way toward the light.

When she arrived at the front door of a tiny house at the foot of a pine tree, she managed a faint knock. No one heard her. "Open the door!" she cried, as loudly as she could. "I'm starving. I need food!"

The Ant and the Cricket

The singing stopped, and an ant peered out the window. "Who's out there?" he asked.

"It's me—the cricket," the cricket said. "I'm cold and hungry, and I have no place to go." She sneezed.

"We worked hard all summer while you sang songs," said the ants, gathering around the window.

"Sorry, there's no free food here," said an ant, munching on a corn kernel.

Then they went back to their singing.

"Poor me," the cricket moaned, wishing she had collected food while it was plentiful. She collapsed on the doorstep.

The next day, a small ant peered out the window. "That lazy cricket's still here!" he cried. "And she looks too weak to move."

At last, the ants took pity on the cricket and, gathering all their strength, they carried her into their home. They fed her until she gained her strength back, and then invited her to stay for the rest of the winter—under one condition: She'd have to serve them all their food until the first signs of spring.

Insects

Whether they love them or scream at their sight, all children are fascinated by bugs. Take your child on an expedition to learn more about these six-legged creatures, and watch new friendships form. Search for these insects under rocks, in the garden, near a pond, or in the darkness after dusk. Your child can catch fireflies in a jar (poking holes in the lid, of course) and keep them by the bed for a night, shedding light on fears both of insects and the dark.

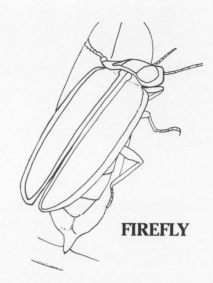

FIREFLY

GRASSHOPPER

PRAYING MANTIS

BUMBLEBEE

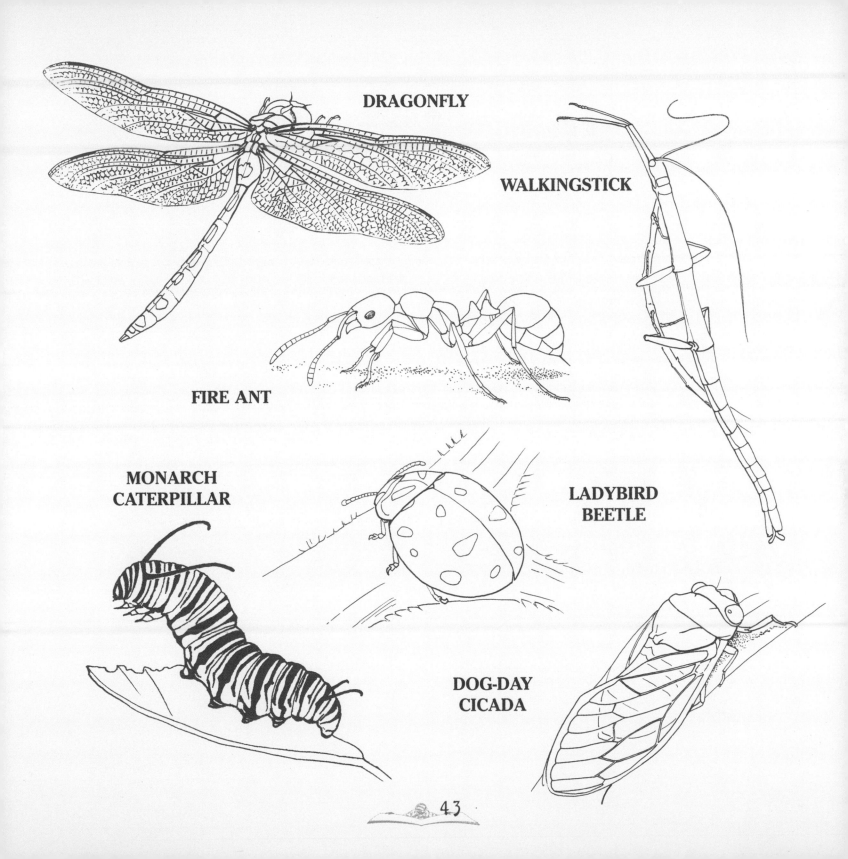

DRAGONFLY

WALKINGSTICK

FIRE ANT

MONARCH
CATERPILLAR

LADYBIRD
BEETLE

DOG-DAY
CICADA

Insect Collecting

Of all the animals on the earth, there are none more plentiful than bugs. You and your child can find thousands of varieties of bugs in your very own backyard or local park. The hunt is only half the fun because some bugs make fine pets, even if only briefly.

EARTHWORMS
jar, loose soil, water, leaves, flashlight, red plastic wrap

1. Fill a jar about three-quarter's full with soil, adding a little water to create a moist consistency. Do not pack the dirt. Put a few leaves on top.
2. Worms are found most easily in the dark after a rainstorm. They tend to stay in damp, cool places, so check underneath rocks and logs. Put the flashlight in red plastic wrap since worms are less sensitive to red light. Carefully scoop up worms with your hands and place them into the jar. Wash your hands afterwards.
3. Put the worms in a dark place, like a closet, for a few days to let them settle down. When you take them out again, they will have started their intricate burrowing. You can add cabbage leaves or other leafy vegetables for food, but be sure to remove rotting food periodically.

4. Keep the jar in a dark place in between viewings and keep the soil moist. Earthworms can have as many as 15 babies about every 5 weeks and can live up to 10 years! It will be necessary to release worms back outside as they multiply.

FIREFLIES
jar, flashlight

1. On a summer evening, look for the telltale green light of the firefly. If it's moving around (meaning that the fly is male), study the pattern of the light and try to imitate it with your flashlight. He will fly up to you, thinking you are a female firefly answering his light signal.
2. Try to catch the fly with cupped hands. This may take some time, but fireflies tend to be rather friendly, at least compared to other bugs.
3. If you manage to catch one, place it carefully in a jar, covering the open end. Only keep it there a little while because fireflies do not survive long in captivity.

An Alphabet
by Edward Lear

A

A was once an apple pie,
Pidy
Widy
Tidy
Pidy
Nice insidy
    Apple Pie!

B

B was once a little bear,
Beary!
Wary!
Hairy!
Beary!
Taky cary!
Little Bear!

C

C was once a little cake,
Caky
Baky
Maky
Caky
Taky Caky,
Little Cake!

D

D was once a little doll,
Dolly
Molly
Polly
Nolly
Nursy Dolly
Little Doll!

E

E was once a little eel,
Eely
Weely
Peely
Eely
Twirly, Tweely
Little Eel!

G

G was once a little goose,
Goosy
Moosy
Boosey
Goosey
Waddly-woosy
Little Goose!

F

F was once a little fish,
Fishy
Wishy
Squishy
Fishy
In a Dishy
Little Fish!

H

H was once a little hen,
Henny
Chenny
Tenny
Henny
Eggsy-any
Little Hen?

I

I was once a bottle of ink,
Inky
Dinky
Thinky
Inky
Blacky Minky
Bottle of Ink!

J

J was once a jar of jam,
Jammy
Mammy
Clammy
Jammy
Sweety—swammy
Jar of Jam!

K

K was once a little kite,
Kity
Whity
Flighty
Kity
Out of Sighty—
Little Kite!

L

L was once a little lark,
Larky!
Marky!
Harky!
Larky!
In the Parky,
Little Lark!

M

M was once a little mouse,
Mousey
Bousey
Sousy
Mousy

In the Housy
Little Mouse!

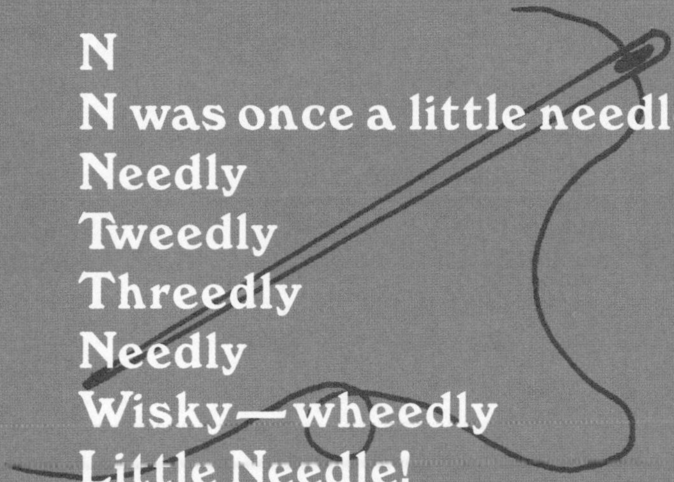

N

N was once a little needle,
Needly
Tweedly
Threedly
Needly
Wisky—wheedly
Little Needle!

O

O was once a little owl,
Owly
Prowly
Howly
Owly
Browny fowly
Little Owl!

P

P was once a little pump,
Pumpy
Slumpy
Flumpy
Pumpy
Dumpy, Thumpy
Little Pump!

Q

Q was once a little quail,
Quaily
Faily
Daily
Quaily
Stumpy-taily
Little Quail!

R

R was once a little rose,
Rosy
Posy
Nosy
Rosy
Blows-y—grows-y
Little Rose!

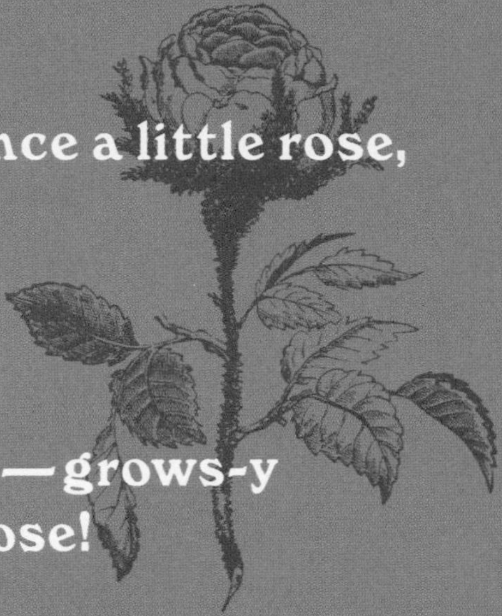

S

S was once a little shrimp,
Shrimpy
Nimpy
Flimpy
Shrimpy
Jumpy—jimpy
Little Shrimp!

T

T was once a little thrush,
Thrushy!
Hushy!
Bushy!
Thrushy!
Flitty—flushy
Little Thrush!

U

U was once a little urn,
Urny
Burny
Turny
Urny
Bubbly—burny
Little Urn!

V

V was once a little vine,
Viny
Winy
Twiny
Viny

Twisty-twiny
Little Vine!

W

W was once a whale,
Whaly
Scaly
Shaly
Whaly
Tumbly-taily
Mighty Whale!

X

X was once a great
    king Xerxes,
Xerxy
Perxy
Turxy
Xerxy
Linxy lurxy
Great King Xerxes!

Y

Y was once a little yew,
Yewdy
Fewdy
Crudy
Yewdy
Growdy, grewdy,
Little Yew!

Z

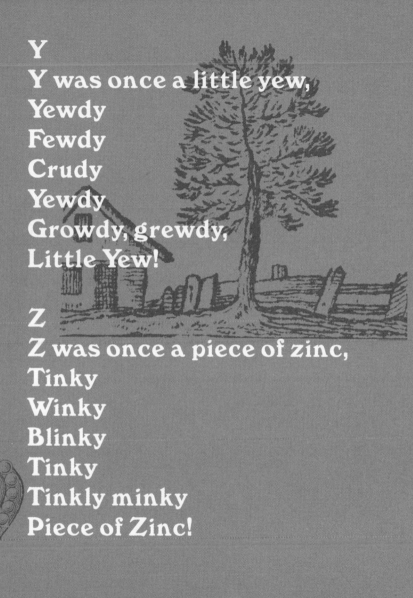

Z was once a piece of zinc,
Tinky
Winky
Blinky
Tinky
Tinkly minky
Piece of Zinc!

So long as enthusiasm
lasts, so long is youth
still with us.

—Anonymous

All the Pretty Little Horses

Hush - a - bye, don't you cry. Go to sleep-y lit -tle ba - by,

Blacks and bays, dap -ples and grays, coach and six-a - lit -tle hor - ses.

Hush - a - bye, don't you cry. Go to sleep-y lit -tle ba - by,

2. When you wake, you shall have all the pretty little horses.
Blacks and bays, dapples and grays, coach and six-a-little horses.
Hush-a-bye, don't you cry. Go to sleep-y little baby.

55

Baa, Baa, Black Sheep

Baa, baa, black sheep,
Have you any wool?
Yes sir, yes sir,
Three bags full;

One for my master,
One for my dame,
But none for the little boy
Who cries in the lane.

Bird Feeders

Making your own bird feeder is not only a good way to help the feathered ones living in your neighborhood, it's also a good way to acquaint your child with Mother Nature. Place the bird feeder near a window or in a tree in a frequented spot near your home. Your child can watch and learn to identify the birds that come to appreciate his or her offering.

HUMMINGBIRD FEEDER
orange, knife

1. Slice an orange in half and pierce it onto a sturdy twig on a tree. The cut side of the orange should face out so that hummingbirds (or butterflies) can easily sip from the orange.

PEANUT BUTTER FEEDER
peanut butter, bird seed, pinecone, string

1. Spread peanut butter in the crevices of a large pinecone.
2. Roll the pinecone in some birdseed, making sure that a significant amount of the seed sticks.
3. Tie a piece of very strong string to the pinecone, and hang it from the branch of a tree near your home.

MILK CARTON FEEDER
1-quart milk carton, bird seed, a small stick, string, scissors

1. Clean and dry the milk carton. Cut out and remove two parallel sides of the carton, leaving about three inches at the bottom, and several inches at the top of each side. The space that is cut out should be large enough for a bird to perch in.
2. Poke a hole through the top of the two sides that are still intact, and run the stick through it.
3. Tie a string to each side of the stick (where it sticks out the sides of the milk carton).
4. Fill the bottom with seed and hang the feeder from a tree branch.

Birds

Birds are nature's musicians, boasting their songs from the tops of trees, telephone poles, lampposts, and piers. Whether you live in the city, the country, or somewhere in between, chances are you encounter at least one of these feathered friends on a daily basis. Introduce your child to the birds that live in your neighborhood, letting him or her hear and enjoy the different songs. In time your child will be able to identify by sound alone the source of the twittering outside the window at the crack of dawn.

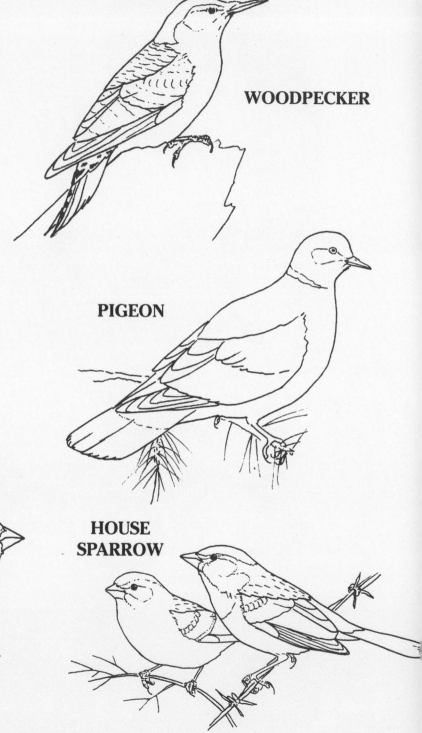

WOODPECKER

PIGEON

HOUSE SPARROW

CARDINAL

HOUSE FINCH

BARN OWL

PURPLE
MARTIN

HUMMINGBIRD

BLUE JAY

ROBIN

61

Peter Piper

a peck of

Peter Piper picked a peck of pickled peppers.

A peck of pickled peppers Peter Piper picked.

If Peter Piper picked a peck of pickled peppers,

Where's the peck of pickled peppers Peter Piper picked?

picked
pickled peppers

Burgers and Unfries

Pretty basic—but I wanted a perfect version. So, I asked Jon, one of our designers, to try it out on his two sons. Kai loved them but not Kojin. Jon gently explained that Kai was born in the Year of the Tiger but Kojin (born in the Year of the Mouse) wasn't a meat eater. Thank goodness for the Macaroni and Cheese recipe that follows.

Burgers

1 lb ground turkey or beef
$1/2$ cup diced onion
$1/4$ cup ketchup
$1/3$ cup milk
$1/2$ cup bread crumbs (see page 94)
1 egg
$1/4$ teaspoon salt
$1/8$ teaspoon pepper
butter (for frying pan method)
4 hamburger rolls

1. Preheat the grill, broiler, or get out the frying pan.
2. In a large bowl, mix meat, onion, ketchup, milk, bread crumbs, egg, salt, and pepper. Divide and shape into four patties.
3. If you are frying, put a pat of butter into a large frying pan over medium-high heat.
4. Grill, broil, or fry about 5 minutes on each side, until meat is no longer pink in the middle.
5. Serve with tomato, onion, or lettuce on rolls—and, of course, unfries!

Serves 4

Unfries

$1^1/2$ lbs baking potatoes (3 large), peeled (or not) and cut into strips
1 tablespoon grated Parmesan cheese
1 tablespoon vegetable oil
$1/4$ teaspoon each salt, garlic powder, paprika, and pepper

1. Preheat oven to 450°F.
2. Combine all ingredients in a bowl. Arrange on a baking sheet.
3. Bake 25 minutes or until brown. Serve with burgers and ketchup.

Serves 4

Macaroni and Cheese

Kids who don't like macaroni and cheese are few and far between. Make them happy with this simple dish or the slightly "jazzed up" macaroni casserole.

6 plus 2 tablespoons butter
1/4 cup plus 2 teaspoons all-purpose flour
3 cups milk
1 1/2 teaspoons dry mustard
1/8 teaspoon cayenne
salt and pepper to taste
1 lb elbow macaroni
3 cups coarsely grated extra sharp
    cheddar cheese (about 12 oz)
1 plus 1/3 cups grated Parmesan
    cheese (about 4 oz)
1 cup bread crumbs (you can use
    cornflakes, matzoh, or saltines,
    crushed in a plastic sandwich bag)

1. In a saucepan, melt 6 tablespoons butter over medium-low heat. Mix in flour and whisk until smooth and bubbly but not brown, about 3 minutes. Continue whisking as you slowly stir in the milk and bring to a gentle boil. Add mustard, cayenne and salt and pepper. Whisk for 5 minutes. Simmer, stirring occasionally, until sauce is thick, about 2 minutes.
2. Cook macaroni in a pot of boiling water for 7 to 8 minutes. Drain.
3. In a bowl combine macaroni, sauce, cheddar cheese, and 1 cup of Parmesan cheese and serve.

Macaroni Casserole

1. Preheat oven to 350°F and butter a 3- to 4-quart casserole dish.
2. Follow steps 1 to 3 above, then pour mixture into the buttered dish.
3. In a bowl, combine bread crumbs, 1 tablespoon of soft butter, and 1/3 cup of Parmesan. Mix well, making sure the butter is spread throughout. Sprinkle mixture on top of casserole and bake 25 to 30 minutes.

Dad's Sandwiches

Franco (my guy) always ate what he made for his son Jay, and this is "guy" food at its easiest and best.

Quick and Easy Tacos

2 to 3 lbs ground turkey or beef
1 package taco seasoning
10 "folded", ready-to-fill taco shells,
   warmed

Toppings:
2 cups cheddar cheese (shredded)
1 small container sour cream
1 tomato (chopped)
1/2 head iceberg lettuce (shredded)
1 jar mild or medium salsa

1. In a large frying pan over medium-high heat, cook the meat until fully browned.
2. Follow the directions on the back of the taco seasoning mix. Add to meat and simmer until seasoned.
3. Put the toppings and meat into separate bowls. Let the kids fill their own tacos, meat first.

Serves 10

Tuna Melt

1 can (6-oz) tuna, drained
2 tablespoons mayonnaise
2 tablespoons butter
4 slices white or sourdough bread
2 slices cheddar cheese

1. Mix tuna and mayonnaise. Heat in microwave for 40 seconds on high.
2. In a small frying pan over medium heat, melt 1/2 tablespoon butter. Place a slice of bread in pan with a slice of the cheddar cheese on top. Cover pan until the cheese melts and the bread is lightly toasted.
3. Put 1/2 of the tuna on top of the cheese and another slice of bread on top. Add 1/2 tablespoon butter, turn and fry on other side. Remove from heat.
4. Repeat for second tuna melt.

Serves 2

The Brave Little Tailor

Once upon a time, in a village at the edge of the forest, a little tailor was sewing a coat for a customer. He was so focused on his work that he forgot to eat his lunch, and by late afternoon he felt starved.

"Strawberry jam for sale!" came a call from the window. "It's the sweetest jam around!"

"Yum," said the tailor, laying down the unfinished coat. "I'd like one jar, please."

He paid for the jam, spread it on a roll, and set it on the counter. "I'll finish the sleeves before eating," he said to himself. "Otherwise, the coat might get sticky."

By the time he finished the sleeves, he was so hungry his stomach was growling like a lion. He went to get the jam-covered roll but was too late—for there, buzzing and squirming in the jam, were seven hungry flies.

Instantly, the tailor raised his hand and slammed it on the flies. What a mess!

When he lifted his sticky hand, he counted: one, two, three,

The Brave Little Tailor

four, five, six, seven flies. They were all dead.

"Seven in one blow!" the little tailor said, impressed with himself. After eating a plain roll, he made himself a cloth belt and, in red thread, embroidered SEVEN IN ONE BLOW across the front. He put it on and admired himself in the mirror.

"I'm much too brave to be a tailor," he said. Then he locked his door and set off to find an adventure. The little tailor had walked less than a mile when one of the king's messengers stopped him by the side of the road.

"Seven in one blow!" the messenger said, staring at the tailor's belt. "I must bring you to the king." And so he did.

"Seven in one blow!" cried the king, as the little tailor stood before him. "Do you suppose you could get rid of the two evil giants that have been threatening the villagers?"

"I suppose so," said the little tailor. "I got rid of seven in one blow—and that's the truth."

The king gave him a sword and sent him into the forest.

The little tailor hadn't gone very far when he heard: *BOOM!*

The Brave Little Tailor

BOOM! BOOM! BOOM! The giants were coming!

Needing time to think, the little tailor scampered up an oak tree and peered out from the branches. The giants sure were ugly, especially when they yawned. One had no teeth and the other only one eye. When the giants reached the foot of the oak tree, they lay down for a nap.

Quietly, the little tailor picked up a pinecone and dropped it— *PLUNK*—onto the toothless giant's nose.

"Stop it!" the toothless giant growled, glaring at his partner.

"Stop what?" asked the one-eyed giant.

The little tailor dropped another pinecone on the toothless giant's nose—*PLUNK!*

"Stop *that!*" the toothless giant roared. He shoved the one-eyed giant, and soon the two of them were engaged in a terrible fight that made the whole forest tremble. Finally, each giant ripped a tree out of the earth—not the tree the tailor was in—and whacked each other until they were both knocked senseless.

"Marvelous work!" cried the king when the little tailor returned, for he had heard the good news. "I shall give you a reward; but first, do you suppose you could get rid of the ferocious unicorn that's been scaring the villagers?"

"I suppose so," said the little tailor. "I got rid of two evil giants and seven in one blow—and that's the truth."

The Brave Little Tailor

So once again, the little tailor set off for the woods. Before long, he heard: *BA-DRUMP! BA-DRUMP!* The unicorn was coming! Like all unicorns, this one had the head and body of a horse, the hind legs of a stag, the tail of a lion, and a horn in the center of its forehead. But unlike most unicorns, which are beautiful and gentle, this one was ferocious and had an exceptionally sharp horn—now pointed directly at the little tailor!

With no time to think and no time to climb a tree, the little tailor fainted to the ground, so instead of running into the little tailor, the unicorn charged—*BOING*—right into a tree. His horn stuck deep into the trunk.

"Now you shall have two rewards!" the king exclaimed. "But first, do you suppose you could get rid of the vicious wild boar that has been seen prowling around the villagers' homes?"

"I suppose so," said the little tailor. "I got rid of a ferocious unicorn, two evil giants, and seven in one blow—and that's the truth."

So a third time the little tailor went back to the woods. He'd gone less than two steps when he heard: *SNORT, SNORT!* The wild boar was coming! And it was the meanest beast the tailor had ever seen.

"Yikes!" the little tailor cried, and ran as fast as his little legs would carry him. The wild boar followed right behind, nipping at

The Brave Little Tailor

his heels. The little tailor saw a hut and ran into it. But before he could slam the door, the wild boar came in behind him. The little tailor saw a little window and climbed through it. Then he hurried around to the front and locked the door. Luckily, the wild boar was too large to fit through the little window.

"Now you shall have three rewards!" cried the king. "But first, do you suppose you could get rid of a dragon that—"

"I'm *sure* I could," said the little tailor, "whatever it is. I got rid of a vicious wild boar, a ferocious unicorn, two evil giants, and seven in one blow—and that's the truth. But if you don't mind, I'd like to take my reward and go home. I have some work to finish."

So the exhausted little tailor carried three bags of gold back to his shop. Before getting back to his sewing, he took off the belt that said SEVEN IN ONE BLOW and hung it in the back of his closet. "From now on, I think I'll stay home," he said to himself. Then he curled up on his bed and took a long, peaceful nap.

And to this day, the dragon the king wanted him to get rid of is still roaming around in the woods.

Georgy Porgy

Georgy Porgy,
pudding and pie,

Kissed the girls and
made them cry.

When the boys
came out to play,

Georgy Porgy ran away.

Froggy Went a-Courtin'

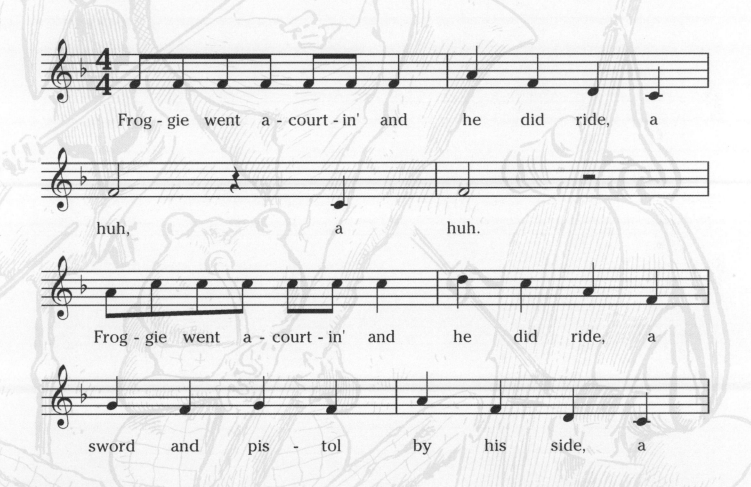

Frog - gie went a - court - in' and he did ride, a

huh, a huh.

Frog - gie went a - court - in' and he did ride, a

sword and pis - tol by his side, a

Froggy Went a-Courtin'

huh. a huh. Well, he
rode down to Miss Mous - e's door, a
huh, a huh. Well, he rode down to Miss
Mous - e's door, where he had of - ten
been be - fore, a huh, a huh.

Froggy Went a-Courtin'

3. He took Miss Mousie on his knee,
   a-huh, a-huh,
   He took Miss Mousie on his knee,
   Said, "Miss Mousie will you marry
   me?" A-huh, a-huh.

4. "I'll have to ask my Uncle Rat, etc.
   See what he will say to that," etc.

5. "Without my Uncle Rat's consent,
   I would not marry the President."

6. Well, Uncle Rat laughed and shook
   his sides,
   To think his niece would be a bride.

7. Well, Uncle Rat rode off to town
   To buy his niece a wedding gown.

8. "Where will the wedding supper be?"
   "Way down yonder in a hollow tree."

9. "What will the wedding supper be?"
   "A fried mosquito and a roasted flea."

10. First to come in were two little ants,
    Fixing around to have a dance.

11. Next to come in was a bumble bee,
    Bouncing a fiddle on his knee.

12. Next to come in was a fat sassy lad,
    Thinks himself as big as his dad.

13. Thinks himself a man indeed,
    Because he chews the tobacco weed.

14. And next to come in was a big tomcat,
    He swallowed the frog and the mouse
    and the rat.

15. Next to come in was a big old snake,
    He chased the party into the lake.

16. There's bread and honey on the shelf,
    If you want anymore just sing it yourself.

Daisy, Daisy

While the goddesses of ancient Greece wore daisy chains, divinity is not a prerequisite to wearing these beautiful strings of flowers. Take your child to an open field to pick fresh daisies. Use some to make daisy chains for the head or neck. Teach your child how to say "He/she loves me, He/she loves me not" with the petals. Then take some home to press and dry for making special art for Mom.

DAISY CHAINS
daisies

1. Break the stems so that they are about an inch long.
2. Using your fingernail, make a small slit near the middle of the stem.
3. Thread the stem of the second daisy through the slit of the first. The head of the second flower should rest against the stem of the first.
4. Make a slit on the second flower and thread a third flower through. Continue threading daisies until you run out of daisies or the chain reaches the desired length.
5. Tie the stems on each end together to close your chain.

PRESSED DAISIES
daisies, white drawing paper, heavy books, glue, construction paper or stationery, crayons

1. Place freshly picked daisies between two sheets of drawing paper. Press between the pages of a heavy book. Place more books on top. Set in a warm, dry place for about a week.
2. Carefully remove the flowers from the paper.
3. Let your child paste onto construction paper and complete the scene with crayons. Or let your child glue daisies to the edges of stationery for pretty floral notes for their favorite people.

Knock knock!

Knock Knock!

Who's there?

Boo.

Boo who?

What's the matter?

Don't cry!

Knock Knock!

Who's there?

Atch.

Atch who?

God bless you! Are you getting a cold?

Knock Knock!

Who's there?

Cows.

Cows who?

Cows don't go who.

Cows go moo!

Knock Knock!

Who's there?

You.

You who?

Are you calling me?

Knock Knock?

> *Who's there?*

Ya.

> *Ya who?*

Yahoo? Are you
a cowboy?

Knock Knock!

> *Who's there?*

A little old lady.

> *A little old lady who?*

I didn't know
you can yodel.

Knock Knock!

> *Who's there?*

Banana.

> *Banana who?*

Knock Knock!

> *Who's there?*

Banana.

> *Banana who?*

Knock Knock!

> *Who's there?*

Orange.

> *Orange who?*

Orange you glad I
didn't say banana?

Who's there?

85

Knight for a Day

Children like to try on different hats—they like to be kings one day and knights the next. Here is an easy paper hat that can serve as a costume when imaginations take over. Add a broomstick horse and a crafty sword, and your child can defend his or her imaginary kingdom for hours.

PAPER HAT

11 x 17-inch sheet of paper

1. Fold the paper in half to $8^{1}/_{2}$ x 11 inches.
2. With the creased side at the top, fold the two top corners to meet in the middle so that the paper looks like the top of a giant arrow.
3. There should be a rectangular portion underneath the triangular portion of your arrow-top. Fold up one rectangular flap and crease at the bottom of the triangle. Turn over and repeat with the other flap.
4. Decorate with crayons or glue on a feather or a leaf.

PAPER SWORD

2 empty paper towel rolls, masking tape, scissors, aluminum foil

1. Flatten the paper towel rolls. Tape edges closed to hold flattened shape.
2. Tape the ends of two rolls together.
3. Trim off two corners on one end to create a point on the sword. Tape edges together.
4. Wrap the sword with aluminum foil to make a steely blade!

BROOMSTICK HORSE

small broomstick, white athletic sock, tissue, rubber band, marker, scissor, paper, glue, yarn

1. Stuff the foot portion of the sock with tissue.
2. Pull the tube portion over the non-bristle end of the broomstick and secure with a rubber band. The sock should now look something like a horse's head.
3. Decorate the head with the marker, creating eyes, nose, and mouth. You can also glue on paper ears and a yarn mane.

Puss in Boots

Once upon a time, a miller died and left his eldest son a mill, his second son a donkey, and his third son a cat.

"What a useless cat," the third son said, watching it sleep in the grass. "All it does is sleep, sleep, *sleep*! At least my brothers can earn a living with a mill and a donkey. But who ever heard of earning a living with a cat? I might as well just eat it and be full for a day!"

"No way!" the cat exclaimed, springing to its feet. "Fetch me a pair of boots and a sack, Master, and I'll see that you have great riches in no time."

The young man stared at the cat, for he had never heard it speak.

"The name is Puss," the cat said. "And I wear size six in a boot."

The young man did as he was asked and was impressed at how charming Puss looked in his shiny new boots.

Quick as a flash, Puss scampered into the woods, caught a rabbit, and stuffed it into his sack. Then he went to the palace and presented it to the king. "Sire, the Marquis of Carabas sends you this fine rabbit," he announced.

Though the king had never heard of the Marquis of Carabas

Puss in Boots

(Puss had made him up), he did love rabbit. "Please thank the Marquis," he said, handing Puss a gold coin.

Over the next few days, Puss brought the king a quail, a trout, and a pheasant. "Be sure to thank the Marquis," the king said each time, handing Puss a gold coin.

Meanwhile, back at the cottage, which they had bought with two gold coins, the young man was amused. "Me? The Marquis of Carabas?" he said, chuckling. But he was grateful for the gold.

One morning, Puss heard that the king and his pretty daughter would be going out for a drive along the river. "Hurry, Master!" he cried. "Jump in the river and act like you're drowning."

By the time the king's carriage rolled toward the river, the young man was splashing and spluttering in the water.

"Help!" Puss cried, waving in front of the carriage. "The Marquis of Carabas is drowning! Thieves stole his clothes!" (Puss had really hidden them under a rock.)

Recognizing Puss, the king shouted orders to his men: "Rescue the Marquis at once! Send for some fine new clothes."

Before long, the young man was dressed in satins and silks. The king was impressed by how handsome he looked—but not as impressed as the princess. "Join us on our drive," she said shyly, making room on the seat. The young man climbed into the carriage and found the princess to be quite charming.

Puss in Boots

Puss dashed ahead and came to an orchard. "When the king asks," he said to the harvesters, "tell him this orchard belongs to the Marquis of Carabas."

"Okay," the harvesters said.

Minutes later, when the king asked who the orchard belonged to, the harvesters answered, "The Marquis of Carabas." The king raised an eyebrow.

By then, Puss was up ahead, giving orders to a group of fishermen.

"Who owns these boats?" the king called out when the carriage rolled by the dock.

"The Marquis of Carabas," answered the fishermen. The king beamed at the young man sitting next to his daughter.

Soon Puss came to an ogre's castle that was every bit as elegant as the king's palace. The ogre also owned all the surrounding land.

"Who have we here?" the ogre sneered, inspecting Puss from head to boot tip.

"The name is Puss, and I'm here to find out if the rumors are true. Can you really turn yourself into a lion?"

"Grrr!" roared the ogre, and he instantly became a ferocious lion.

"Incr-r-redible," Puss said, trembling. He was relieved when the ogre became himself again. "But I'll bet you couldn't turn yourself into a tiny mouse."

Puss in Boots

Puss in Boots

"Oh yeah?" the ogre sneered. Instantly, a tiny mouse stood in his place. Quick as a flash, Puss gobbled him up.

By the time the king's carriage arrived at the castle, Puss was standing proudly at the front gate. "Welcome, Sire, to the home of the Marquis of Carabas!"

"What a magnificent home!" the king said admiringly.

"Why thank you," said the young man, suddenly feeling like a real Marquis. "Won't you come in?"

"Not until you agree to marry me," the princess said, blushing.

"Splendid idea!" said the king, overjoyed. "I'd be honored to have the Marquis of Carabas as my son-in-law."

"I'd be honored to marry your daughter," said the Marquis, taking the princess's hand.

They were married the next day. The Marquis's brothers, who came as guests, were amazed at their brother's success.

"I have the cat to thank," the Marquis of Carabas said, smiling proudly at Puss. "A mill and a donkey are nice, but a cat in boots—now, that's a real treasure!"

After the ceremony, the Marquis appointed Puss Lord of the Castle and proclaimed him the Smartest Cat in the Land. And Puss spent the rest of his days sleeping to his heart's content, without fear of being eaten by man or beast.

Easy Magic

All kids think their fathers have superpowers—prove them right while they still believe in magic. The following magic tricks are easy and safe, but they will require some practicing. The disappearing coin trick has been around forever and does not cease to amaze. The heads or tails trick is a great one to bet on. Tell your child that he or she has to clean up or eat tons of vegetables if you can guess heads or tails correctly—and you always will.

COIN-SWALLOWING ELBOW
a coin and some flair

1. Show your audience the coin in your right hand. Bend your left elbow, placing your left hand on the back of your neck. With your right hand, rub the coin vigorously back and forth into the elbow. After some time, say that the trick works better with the other hand and drop the coin on the table.
2. Pick the coin up with your right hand, and *pretend* to quickly put it into the left hand. Then start rubbing the imaginary coin into the right elbow, while pressing the coin in your right hand into the back of your neck or under your shirt collar.

3. Expose both empty hands with a grand *"ta da!"*

HEADS OR TAILS?
quarter, improved upon

1. Using a hammer and a nail, make a nick on one side of a quarter. Note what side you make this on.
2. Practice dropping the quarter on a table—it will make a duller sound when it lands on the side with the nick. Memorize the sound!
3. Tell your child you can guess heads or tails correctly every time. Let your child spin the quarter or toss it over the table. Listen for the difference and amaze your child.

Marshmallow Fun

Children love to build things, play with their food, and eat sweets, so you can imagine how much fun they'll have with these activities. Learning to juggle with marshmallows is safe and a whole bag of fun. If juggling on a relatively clean surface, the five-second rule applies—food on the floor for no more than five seconds can still be eaten!

MARSHMALLOW CONSTRUCTION
bag of marshmallows, toothpicks, clean surface

1. Use toothpicks to connect marshmallows together.
2. Build a marshmallow family, a tower, or simply the longest chain of marshmallows imagined.
3. When tired of building, eat.

CHILD-PROOF JUGGLING
bag of large marshmallows

1. Take one marshmallow and practice throwing it in a low arc from one hand to the other. Keep practicing until you can transfer the marshmallow from one hand to the other keeping the same low arc, with few mistakes.
2. Hold a marshmallow in each hand. Throw one marshmallow in a low arc to the other hand. As the first marshmallow starts to drop, throw the second marshmallow in a low arc to the other hand. Practice until you have the rhythm.
3. Add the third marshmallow to the mix. Hold two marshmallows in one hand and one marshmallow in the other. Using the hand holding two marshmallows, throw one marshmallow in a low arc to the other hand. As the first marshmallow reaches the top of the arc, throw the marshmallow in the other hand, again in a low arc. Just as the second marshmallow reaches the top of the arc and the first marshmallow lands in your hand, throw the last marshmallow.
4. Remember the five-second rule.

There is no heavier
burden than potential.

—Charlie Brown

Little Tom Tucker

Little Tom Tucker
Sings for his supper.
What shall he eat?
White bread and butter.
How will he cut it
Without e'er a knife?
How will he be married
Without e'er a wife?

The Mouse and the Clock

Hickory, dickory, dock!

The mouse ran up the clock;

The clock struck one,

And down he run,

Hickory, dickory, dock!

The Emperor's New Clothes

Once upon a time there lived an emperor who loved clothes. The only reason he ever went to the theater, to banquets, or on strolls was to show off his latest outfit. He spent more time trying on his clothes and standing in front of the mirror than he did taking care of his country. He had an outfit for every hour of the day!

One day, two men—one tall and thin like a pencil, the other short and squat like a bullfrog—arrived at the palace. They said they were weavers, though they were really swindlers, people who trick other people.

"We can weave a golden fabric more beautiful and exquisite than any you can imagine," said the taller swindler.

"And most amazing of all," said the shorter swindler, "the fabric is invisible to anyone stupid. Only smart people can see it."

"Hmm," the Emperor said, scratching his chin. "A beautiful fabric only smart people can see? Make me a new outfit at once!" he demanded. He paid the swindlers a large sum and ordered that a weaving room be prepared.

 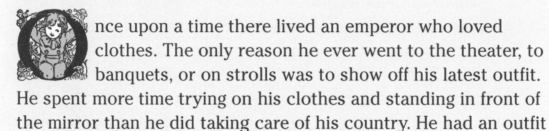

The Emperor's New Clothes

Two great looms and a case of golden thread were ordered, and soon the swindlers got to work—*pretending* to weave the fine fabrics. They were really weaving nothing at all and had stuffed the golden thread into their bags.

For the next three days, the swindlers pretended to slave away at the empty looms while the impatient Emperor tried to be patient. "I can't take it any more!" he finally shouted. "I must have a peek at the new fabric." But as he strutted toward the door of the weaving room, he began to feel nervous.

"What if *I* can't see the fabric?" he thought. "After all, it's a special material that only smart, interesting people can see." He knew he was smart and interesting—but was he smart and interesting *enough* to see the fabric? By now, everyone in town had heard about the magical powers of the fabric and was anxious to find out which of their neighbors could see it and which of them couldn't. If a rumor got around that the Emperor couldn't see it, he'd be the laughingstock of the town. Just to be safe, the Emperor sent his most reliable adviser to see it first.

"Have you ever seen such lovely fabric?" the taller swindler asked the adviser as he pretended to hold up a section.

The Emperor's New Clothes

"I, I'm speechless," the adviser said, reaching for his glasses. But even with his glasses, he couldn't see a thing.

"I must be stupid!" the adviser thought with surprise. "But if the Emperor finds out, I'll lose my job." He forced a smile and lied. "It's absolutely fabulous, and the patterns are charming." Then he hurried off to tell the Emperor the exact same thing.

After another week, the Emperor became fidgety. "I've ordered two new cases of golden thread," he said to his oldest and wisest lord. "They must be near done." But the Emperor was still a bit hesitant to check on the weavers himself. He sent the lord instead.

"I'll bet you've never seen such magnificent beauty," the shorter swindler said to the lord, pretending to stroke the fine fabric.

"I can't see a thing," the lord thought to himself, though he knew he was no fool. "But if the Emperor finds out I'll lose my job." So, the lord praised the swindlers' work. "It's marvelously elegant," he lied. Then he hurried off to tell the Emperor the exact same thing.

Soon, the Emperor couldn't bear the suspense any longer. He gathered all the advisers, lords, and ladies of the court together and led them to the weaving room.

"My lords and ladies, have you ever seen such a remarkable design?" said the taller swindler.

The Emperor's New Clothes

"Or such truly original colors?" said the shorter swindler. The Emperor was horrified! He couldn't see a thing.

"I mustn't let anyone know that I'm stupid," he thought. "Otherwise, I'll be tossed off the throne—maybe even out of the country!" The advisers, lords, and ladies of the court complimented the swindlers on their wonderful work. (They were pretending, of course!)

"Superb!" the Emperor said. "I'll be honored to wear them in the great parade." The parade was to take place the following day. Since everyone else could see the fabric, he'd just have to trust them. He felt sure it would impress the townspeople as well—at least the smart, interesting ones.

The swindlers burned candles all that night so everyone would think they were working hard to finish up the Emperor's new clothes. Early the next morning, the advisers, lords, and ladies of the court escorted the Emperor to the weaving room.

"Charming! Delightful!" everyone cried as the swindlers held up each garment. But no one saw a thing!

"We're thrilled you're pleased, Your

The Emperor's New Clothes

Majesty," the swindlers said as the Emperor undressed. Then they pretended to help him dress in his pretend new clothes. When they were finished, the Emperor stood proudly in his plain old underwear.

The parade soon began.

"Look at those magnificent clothes!" the townspeople cried. "What lovely colors and patterns!" Nobody dared to admit they couldn't see the new clothes at all—except for the children.

"But he has nothing on but his underwear!" said a giggling boy.

"Papa, his legs are as hairy as yours!" said a giggling girl.

"Mama, look at the king's big belly!" said another boy, who puffed out his own belly to imitate the Emperor.

"I see the Emperor's belly button, I see the Emperor's belly button," a group of children began to chant.

The children's giggles and chants made too much sense to be ignored by the adults, who also began to point and laugh.

The poor Emperor was so embarrassed he ran straight home, one hand over his chest and the other over his belly button. And from that day forth, he always wore plain, gray suits.

Animal

Why did the chicken
cross the road?

> *To get to the
> other side.*

Where do sheep
get haircuts?

> *At a baa-baa shop.*

What did the rooster's
ghost say every
morning at sunrise?

> *Cock-a-doodle-boo!*

Were do cows go
to see art?

> *Moo-seums.*

What do frogs order
at restaurants?

> *Hamburgers and flies.*

What do you say to a
bird on its birthday?

> *Happy Bird-day!*

What do birds say on Halloween?

Trick or tweet!

What has the head of a dog, the tail of a dog, but is not a dog?

A puppy.

What keys are too big to put in your pocket?

Donkeys, turkeys, and monkeys.

If 1 pig, 2 cows, 5 chickens, 3 sheep, and 1 big horse all got under one tiny umbrella, how many animals would get wet?

None. It's not raining!

If a rooster laid a white egg and a brown egg, what color chicks would hatch?

None. Roosters don't lay eggs, hens do.

Jokes

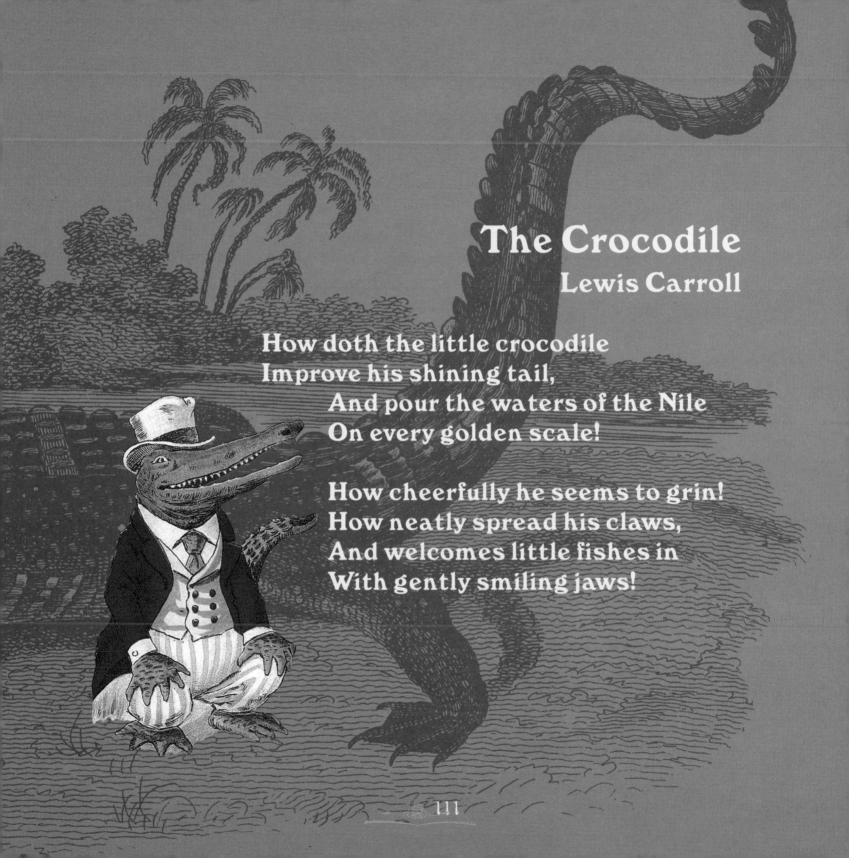

The Crocodile
Lewis Carroll

How doth the little crocodile
Improve his shining tail,
And pour the waters of the Nile
On every golden scale!

How cheerfully he seems to grin!
How neatly spread his claws,
And welcomes little fishes in
With gently smiling jaws!

Kite Tips

Go fly a kite! You have to do this at least once with your young child. There is something so great about a colorful kite soaring high above on a beautiful day. Will it reach the clouds? Choose a wide open space—young children tend to be enthralled for a while and then lose interest. They can at least run around while you stand there with the string, letting your mind soar for a bit longer.

1. Go buy a kite. Cheap and simple ones are readily available. It will fly better and everyone will be happier.

2. A simpler kite is better for novices. Delta-wings tend to be better choices than diamonds, boxes, or other more interesting designs because those can be unpredictable at first.

3. Sunny days with a gentle breeze are the best for flying kites.

4. Choose a place that's clear of trees and other obstructions. Good places are beaches or wide-open fields.

5. Begin by facing the wind and holding the kite up. As the wind starts to push against the kite, release a bit of line. Keep the line tight, releasing a little a a time, until the kite flies high.

6. If the kite begins to free-fall, you can regain control by moving in the direction of the plummet, taking in some line. If this doesn't help, try adding cord to the tail of the kite. If the kite keeps falling backwards, trim the tail.

7. Remember to let your child have a turn with the kite!

Dance to Your Daddy

Dance to your dad-dy, my lit-tle lad-die, Dance to your dad-dy,

my __ lit-tle lamb. You shall get a fish-ie on a lit-tle dish-ie,

You shall get a fish-ie when the boat comes in. Dance to your dad-dy,

my lit-tle lad-die, Dance to your dad-dy, my __ lit-tle lamb.

Beauty and the Beast

Once upon a time many years ago, there lived a rich ship merchant who had three sons and three daughters. His youngest daughter, Beauty, was the loveliest, which is how she got her name. Unlike her snooty sisters, Beauty loved to read, listen to music, and help around the mansion.

One night, the merchant's ships drifted away in a horrendous storm, making him a poor man. The following day, the family moved to a small, run-down farm.

"It's dirty here!" the oldest sister whined.

"It stinks!" the middle sister complained.

But Beauty was happy helping her father and brothers with the chores.

One day, the merchant heard that one of his ships had been found. Before setting off for the harbor, he asked his daughters what they wanted from town.

"A fancy dress," said the oldest sister.

"Silk hair ribbons," said the middle sister.

"A rose," said Beauty, "if you see one."

Beauty and the Beast

Their father's journey was a disaster; his ship sank before he arrived, and he got lost in the forest on his way home. As darkness fell, he saw a light in the distance and rode toward it. Soon, he found himself in front of a magnificent palace. Hungry and exhausted, he tied up his horse and knocked on the door. When no one answered, he walked right in.

Though the palace seemed deserted, supper was waiting on the table. He gobbled it up and fell asleep at the table. He awoke at sunrise, and found a hearty breakfast before him!

Before returning to his horse, the merchant plucked a rose for Beauty— and heard a frightful roar. A horrible beast was heading toward him.

"Ungrateful man!" the beast growled. "I gave you food and shelter, and you thank me by stealing a rose—my very favorite flower! For that I must kill you!"

"I, I only picked one rose, for my daughter Beauty," the merchant explained.

Beauty and the Beast

"Then I'll kill *her*," roared the beast, "if you can get her to come. If not, I'll kill you. Come back in three months!"

The merchant found his way home and told his children what had happened.

"We'll kill that awful beast," said his sons. But their father refused to let them go.

"It's all Beauty's fault," said the oldest sister.

"All for that stupid rose," said the middle sister.

For the first time, Beauty agreed with her sisters and insisted on returning to the beast's palace with her father three months later.

"Did your father make you come?" the beast roared as the three of them ate lunch.

"No," said Beauty. "It was my idea since I asked him to bring me the rose." She couldn't look the beast in the eye, for he was much too ugly.

After lunch, Beauty's father begged her to return home with him, but she stubbornly refused. So after a tearful good-bye, the merchant set off for the farm.

As she wandered around the beast's palace, Beauty felt sad and lonesome. Suddenly, she spied a sign on a door that said Beauty's Room. She opened the door and gasped, for it was the most beautiful room she'd ever seen. The wallpaper and bed-

spread were patterned with roses, and the shelves were filled with books she had never read.

"You're now the queen of the palace," the beast said, startling Beauty, for she hadn't seen him standing in the doorway. "Anything you wish for will be yours."

"I wish to see my poor father," Beauty said, stubbornly.

The beast handed her a magic mirror, which showed her father arriving home safely.

"Thank you," Beauty said, as the image melted away. She smiled for the first time all day.

"Would you mind if—" the beast began.

"What?" Beauty asked, surprised to see the beast's shy side.

"If I-I-I dine with you tonight," the beast finished.

"Not at all," said Beauty, grateful to have company.

When Beauty came down to supper, her favorite music was playing and her favorite meal was on the table.

"How did you know what I liked?" she asked the beast.

"I didn't," the beast said with surprise. "Mozart and macaroni and cheese are my favorites too."

After supper, the beast looked Beauty in the eye. "Do you think I'm terribly ugly?" he asked.

"Yes," Beauty said, unable to lie. "But I know you have a good heart."

Beauty and the Beast

"Then will you marry me?"

"*No!*" Beauty exclaimed in surprise, then wished she hadn't been so rude.

Over the next few months, Beauty began to enjoy living in the beast's palace. She read, listened to music, and wandered around the rose garden. The beast was kind and thoughtful, and seemed to forget his plan to kill her. (Not that Beauty ever reminded him!)

There were always roses in the dining room, and the beast joined Beauty for every meal. They talked about books and music and all their favorite things. The beast was such great company, Beauty soon got used to his ugliness.

But every night, when the beast asked her to marry him, Beauty refused. "I treasure our friendship," she said.

"Then promise you'll never leave me," said the beast.

"I promise," said Beauty, for she hadn't expected to return home anyway. But when the magic mirror showed her father sick in bed, she begged the beast to let her go see her father. "I'll be back in a week," she promised.

"I can't say no to you," said the beast, now

Beauty and the Beast

deeply in love with Beauty. "But if you don't return, I'll die of misery." Then he slipped a magic ring on Beauty's finger. "You'll wake at home tomorrow morning," he explained. "When you're ready to return, lay this ring on your bedside table." And the next morning, Beauty was back at
the farm.

"Beauty!" her father cried, jumping out of bed. Just seeing his youngest daughter alive cured him at once.

"Look at you! Where did you get such beautiful clothes?" asked the oldest sister.

"I thought you were going to be killed," said the middle sister.

Beauty just smiled secretly—for she now realized she was in love with the beast.

Despite her feelings, Beauty was needed at the farm, since her brothers had left for the army. So she stayed longer than a week.

One night, she dreamt that the beast was lying half-dead in the rose garden. Waking in tears, she laid the magic ring on the bedside table and fell asleep again. The next morning, she woke up in the beast's palace—but the beast was nowhere in sight.

She ran out to the rose garden and found the beast lying half-dead on the ground, just as he'd been in her dream. She filled a bucket with water and dumped it over his head.

The beast opened his eyes. "You forgot your promise, Beauty,"

Beauty and the Beast

he said weakly. "And now I'm dying. Love is so painful."

"But it's not!" Beauty cried. "Love is wonderful—and I know that because I love you and want you to be my husband."

Instantly, the palace blazed with light and music filled the air. And Beauty found herself looking into the eyes of a handsome prince.

"Where's the beast?" she asked looking around her.

"*I* was the beast," said the prince. "You see, a wicked fairy put a spell on me that only a beautiful maiden like you could break—and only if she fell in love with me despite my ugliness." He got up and led Beauty into the palace, where her father and her jealous sisters were waiting.

The following afternoon, Beauty and the prince were married, and they lived happily ever after—talking about books, listening to Mozart, eating macaroni and cheese, and smelling the roses.

Animal Tracks

J ust after a fresh blanket of snow falls is the perfect time to look for animal tracks. Take your child outside and look for interesting indentations in the snow. Your child will marvel at these signs of "invisible visitors," and he or she will feel like real detectives when following the trails. Use the illustrations on these pages to help your child identify the animals that trek around your neighborhood in the wintertime. Go get that polar bear!

DOMESTIC CAT

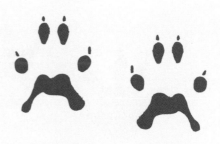

GREY SQUIRREL

PORCUPINE

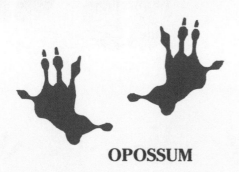

OPOSSUM

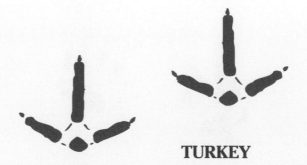

TURKEY

BLACK BEAR

WHITETAIL DEER

BEAVER

MUSKCRAT

JACK RABBIT

OTTER

POLAR BEAR

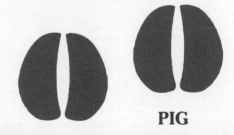

PIG

RACCOON

MOUSE

127

od would a
chuck

How much wood would a woodchuck chuck
If a woodchuck could chuck wood?
A woodchuck would chuck as much wood
As a woodchuck could chuck
If a woodchuck could chuck wood.

could chuck wood?

Take Me Out to the Ball Game

Words by Jack Norworth   Music by Albert von Tilzer

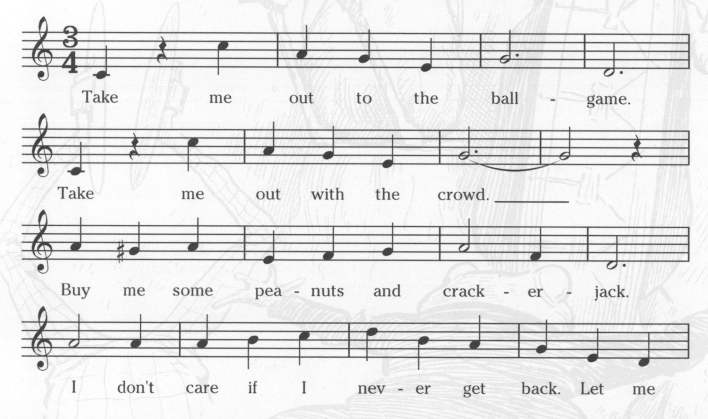

Take me out to the ball - game.

Take me out with the crowd. _____

Buy me some pea - nuts and crack - er - jack.

I don't care if I nev - er get back. Let me

Take Me Out to the Ball Game

root, root, root for the home team. If

they don't win it's a shame. _____ For it's

one, two, three strikes, you're out at the

old ball - game. _____

Rock Skipping

Rock skipping is a very cool "dad" skill. It can take a long time to perfect the throw that causes a rock to skip endlessly across a still lake or pond. Make sure you select a rock that is—above all—flat, relatively smooth, and somewhat round (otherwise you may sabotage your chances of that perfect skip). Follow the instructions below and maybe you'll be able to impress and pass on the technique. Otherwise, stick with rock collecting!

1. Find a still lake or pond and the "perfect" flat rock.
2. Skipping a rock across a lake isn't much different than tossing a Frisbee, except that you want it to skim the surface of the water rather than fly through the air. Hold the rock in your hand as you would a Frisbee, between your thumb and index finger, the rest of your fingers curled in your hand.
3. Toss the rock like a Frisbee, aiming straight across the surface of the water. Envision the rock skimming the surface of the water, rather than skipping (sometimes this helps).

FUN FACTS:
- Diamonds and emeralds are very rare and valuable rocks.
- Talc (soapstone) is the softest rock. Diamonds are the hardest rocks.
- The Egyptians built the pyramids five thousand years ago with limestone. They are still standing today.
- Rocks come in all different colors: black, white, gray, brown, pink, and yellow. See how many different rocks you can find!

Rock Collecting

Rocks are the oldest things your child can collect. Many of them are millions and millions of years old! Let your child start a collection of small rocks from different places he or she visits. Keep the rocks in shoeboxes or egg cartons, sorting them by color, texture, and shape. Teach your child about the different kinds of rocks:

IGNEOUS rocks are formed when molten rock (often called lava) cools and hardens. These rocks are made up of tiny crystals that you can look for when identifying your rock. Granite and basalt are kinds of igneous rocks.

SEDIMENTARY rocks are created by layers upon layers of minerals such as salt and sand, which settle and solidify into rocks. Often these rocks are recognizable by the different colors that you can see in them, which indicate the different layers. Sandstone, shale, and limestone are sedimentary rocks.

METAMORPHIC rocks are igneous and sedimentary rocks that have been subjected to heat and pressure. They may be difficult to identify, but if the rock was originally sedimentary you might be able to see the different layers pressed very tightly together. Marble, soapstone, and slate are metamorphic rocks.

This Old Man

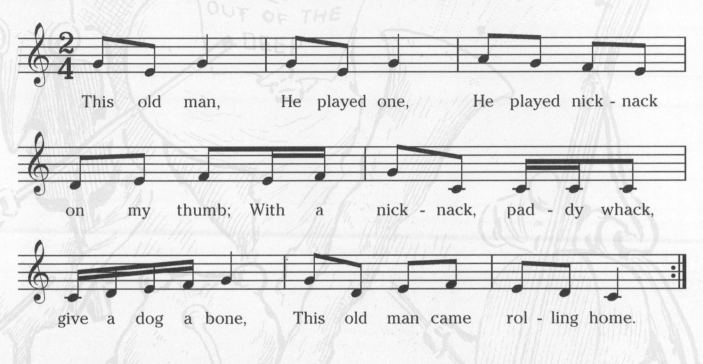

This old man, He played one, He played nick - nack

on my thumb; With a nick - nack, pad - dy whack,

give a dog a bone, This old man came rol - ling home.

2. This old man, he played two,
   He played nick-nack on my shoe;
With a nick-nack paddy whack,
   give a dog a bone,
This old man came rolling home.

3. . . . three . . . on my knee

4. . . . four . . . on my door

5. . . . five . . . on my hive

6. . . . six . . . on my sticks

7. . . . seven . . . up in heaven

8. . . . eight . . . on my gate

9. . . . nine . . . on my spine

10. . . . ten . . . once again

Going Fishing

A goldfish is a wonderful first pet to test the waters with. If your child shows continued interest, you can graduate to a larger tank and more fish. And before that first real fishing trip, let you child try some indoor fishing. By creating your own stock of fish, you can be sure the catch will be plentiful!

A FISH OF YOUR OWN
*goldfish, fish bowl, water
pump filter, food*

1. Purchase a nice, vibrant Betta (Siamese fighting fish) and good sized bowl from your local pet store. It is also a good idea to get a small pump filter to help keep the water clear and to aerate the water.
2. Don't release the fish from the bag of water into the tank right away. Float the bag in the water for about half an hour until the temperature equalizes. This lets the fish adjust to the change.
3. Now for the fun part. Keeping goldfish is pretty easy, so you can teach your child how to take care of the fish. Feed it once or twice a day, depending on what the pet store says, and make sure not to overfeed. Fish always have the appearance of looking hungry, and they will notoriously stuff themselves to death if you let them.

INDOOR FISHING
*stick or small broom handle, string,
large paper clip, construction paper*

1. To make the fishing pole, use the stick or small broom handle, tying string to one end.
2. For a hook, uncoil the paper clip and tie it to the end of the string.
3. For fish, cut 1 x 3-inch strips of different colored construction paper.
4. Fold the paper in half making a V shape.
5. Scatter the Vs on floor, upside down, so that your child can hook them onto the paper clip.

Fish

A fishing trip can be a true bonding experience between a father and his child. On your next trip with your child to the lake or pond, make an activity out of identifying the fish you catch, or the ones you only watch swim by. And more important than the fish are the hours spent waiting, with bait in the water, as you tell your child stories or explore the thoughts that pass through his or her young mind. These are the days and conversations that your child will remember long after the difference between a striped bass and a rainbow trout is forgotten.

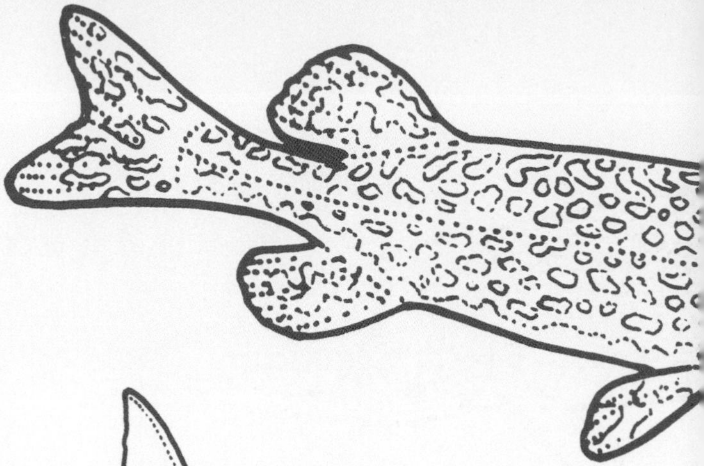

WHITE SHARK

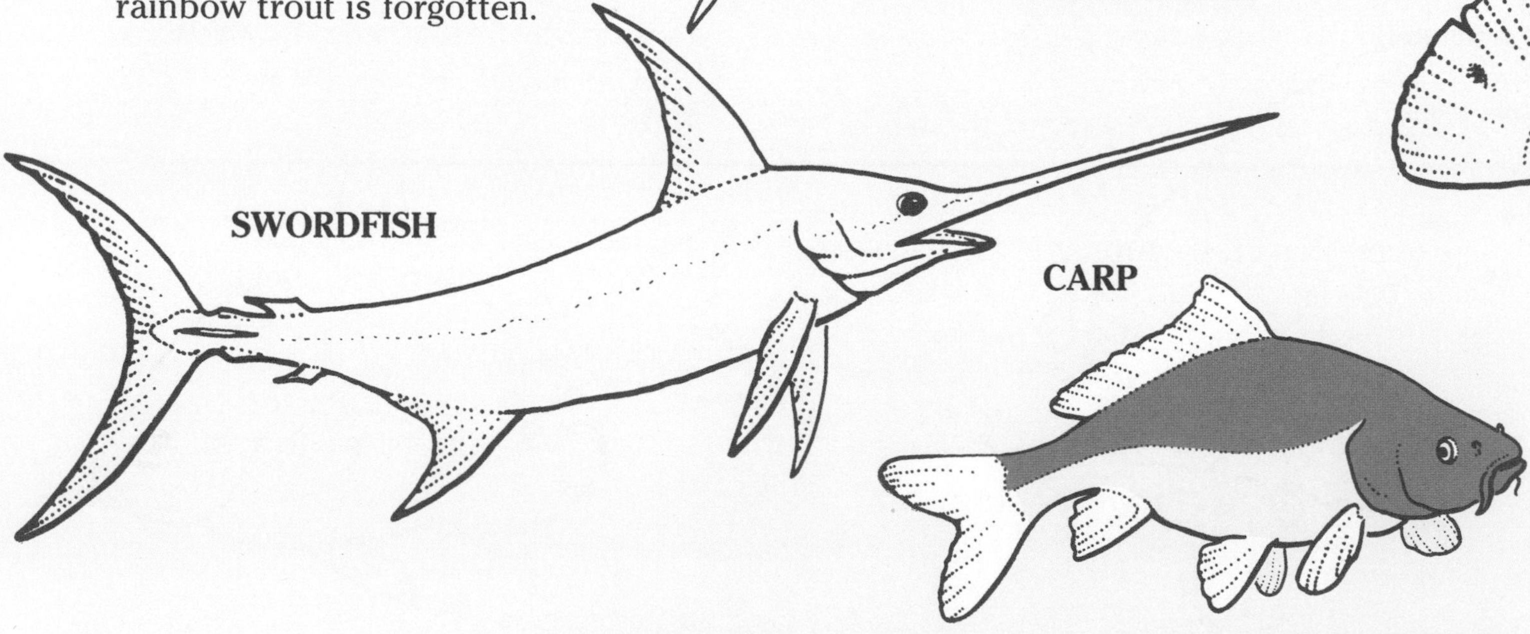

SWORDFISH

CARP

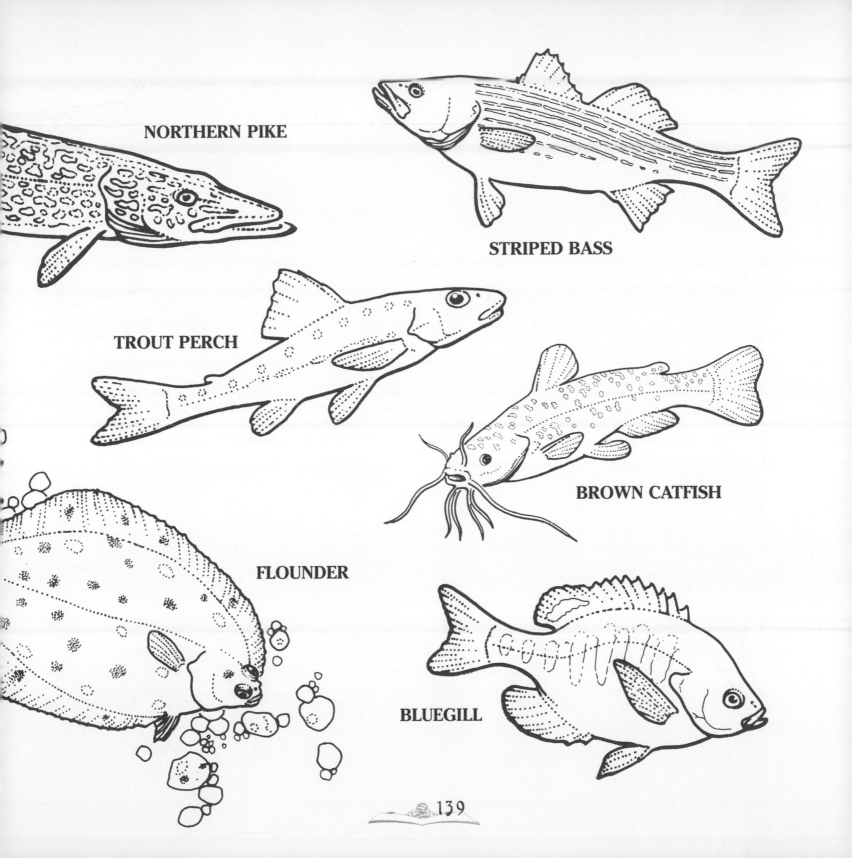

NORTHERN PIKE

STRIPED BASS

TROUT PERCH

BROWN CATFISH

FLOUNDER

BLUEGILL

Down by the Bay

Down   by   the   bay,
echo: Down   by   the

_ where the wa - ter - mel - ons grow,
bay,   where the wa - ter - mel - ons

_ Back to my home, _____ I dare not go,
grow,   Back to my home,   I dare not

_ For   if   I   do,
go,   For   if   I

Down by the Bay

do, My moth - er will say

My moth - er will

say "Did you ev - er see a bear,

Comb - ing his hair?" Down by the bay.

A Day at the Beach

For many children, that first trip to the seashore is the official sign that summer has indeed begun. With crowds of people, a gently crashing surf, and an endless array of exotic things to see and touch, the beach may be one of the most interesting places you can take your child. He or she will be entranced by all the new sights and sounds, but it may also be possible for you to suggest a few activities.

DIGGING FOR TREASURES

Toddlers may be a little intimidated by the sounds and vastness of the ocean on their first visit of the summer. Focus their attention on a little patch of sand. Bury a few of their favorite little toys (figurines or cars) in a circle around them. (For younger children, let the toys stick up a bit out of the sand to make them easier to find.) Provide shovels and let them dig for their treasures.

DIGGING FOR SAND CRABS

Near the water's edge, dig into the sand to about the depth of your hand. You should be able to see sand crabs scurrying about, burrowing under the sand.

SAND ANGELS

Just like snow angels, but in the sand.

BURYING DAD

A favorite. Dig a shallow area to lie in, get comfortable, and let your kids cover you with sand.

WRITING ON SAND

Find a stick on the beach and try scratching giant letters and shapes, tic-tac-toe, and hopscotch in the sand.

FINDING THE BEST SEASHELLS

If you have time, go walking along the beach at low tide and note where the most debris is—these will be the places where the most shells will be collected at high tide. Return to these spots in the morning just after high tide and pick through to find the shells you want to keep.

Sandcastles

No trip to the beach is complete without a sandcastle, or at least a really good attempt at making one. Take along buckets, pails, small hand shovels, and anything that will serve as a mold. Younger children are happy with the simplest of shapes to stomp on. Try building a series of mounds—like an obstacle course for them to weave through without knocking over the shapes. For older children, impress them with these sand structure techniques.

DRIBBLY SAND

1. Select a spot not so close to the shoreline that the waves will reach you, but not too far away, either. Dig a hole until the sand has a very watery consistency.
2. Build a small mound of sand that you can dribble onto.
3. Scoop up a bit of wet sand from the hole. Shape your hand into a fist, hold it a few inches above the mound, and allow sand to "leak" from the bottom of your fist. The wet sand should stick and form dribbly shapes along the sides of the mound.

TOWER BUILDING

1. Squeeze handfuls of wet sand into a pancake shapes, by patting your hands around and using slight pressure. Don't press too hard or the water will be squished out the sides.
2. Stack the cakes on top of one another. As you near the top, begin to use smaller cakes so that the tower will taper off. This will allow for more stability as you and your child carve a fanciful tower with your own decorations.

WALL BUILDING

1. This is good for attaching towers, making stairs, or for creating anything else your imagination compels you to. Using cupped hands, scoop up some wet sand. Hold the sides of the scooped sand between your flattened palms and shake them so that the sand takes a brick-ish shape.
2. Lay the bricks from end to end until you reach your desire length, then begin stacking one on top of the other (a good, fun practice at masonry).

Knots

Knots are an ancient tool and among humankind's oldest inventions. There are all different kinds of knots for many different purposes. It will be interesting for your child to learn about other kinds of knots when learning to tie a shoelace. Meanwhile, try using the bowline knot to create a little leash for your child's stuffed dog or the fisherman's bend to create a pull for a cardboard box wagon.

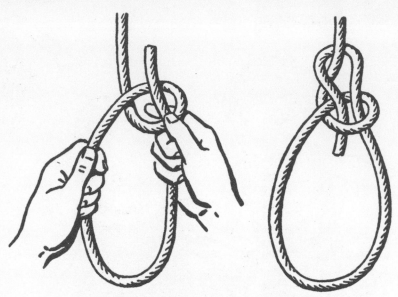

A **BOWLINE KNOT** is used to tie a loop in a rope end.

A **FIGURE EIGHT** is the most commonly used stopper knot to prevent a rope from passing through an opening.

A **BEND** is a type of knot used to unite two rope ends together to lengthen a rope. The **SHEET BEND** is a general utility bend that is easily remembered and can be tied in an instant.

The **CARRICK BEND** is the strongest and most secure of bends.

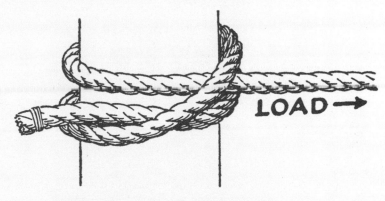

The **FISHERMAN'S BEND** is one of the strongest of all hitches. It is often used to bend (tie) a rope to an anchor—hence the reason for this hitch being termed a bend.

A **HITCH** is a type of knot used to make a rope fast to various objects. The Clove Hitch is the quickest hitch to tie and easiest to remember but is not very secure. It is the most common hitch used in dock lines as a temporary mooring.

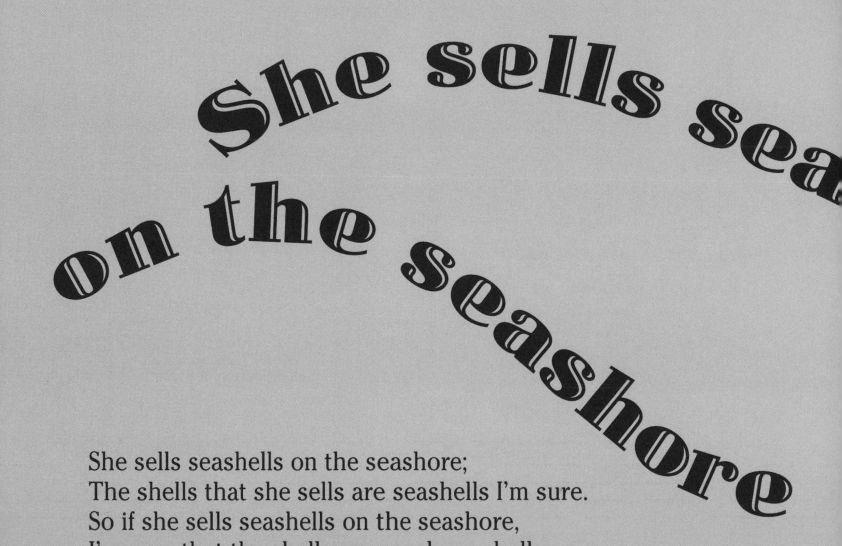

She sells seashells on the seashore;
The shells that she sells are seashells I'm sure.
So if she sells seashells on the seashore,
I'm sure that the shells are seashore shells.

shells

Seashore

Legend has it that if you break the center of a sand dollar, five doves will be released from Heaven to spread goodwill and peace, making it one of the most valuable treasures to be found at the seashore. But there are many other things to be gained there as well. From shells to crustaceans to birds, a trip to the beach can be an educational and memorable experience, as your child learns about the different animals that live in and near the sea. On these pages are some common sights that you and your child can look for on your next visit to the beach—and don't forget to take home a few shells to remember your outing by!

SEAGULL

SEA URCHIN

GHOSTCRAB

HERMIT CRAB

JELLY FISH

ROCK CRAB

SAND DOLLAR

SHRIMP

STARFISH

LOBSTER

SANDPIPER

To unpathed waters,

undreamed shores.

—William Shakespeare

Row, Row, Row Your Boat

Row, row, row your boat

gent - ly down the stream;

Mer - ri - ly, mer - ri - ly, mer - ri - ly, mer - ri - ly,

life is but a dream.

Toy Boats

There are lots of ways to make toy boats and rafts: half a walnut shell can be a sailboat with just a tiny piece of clay in the hull, and a toothpick for a mast. Here are instructions to make a twig raft and a fun and speedy craft capable of maneuvering down any river of imagination or fantasy:

TWIG RAFT

popsicle sticks, glue,
a twig, colored paper

1. Glue the popsicle sticks side by side to create the base of the raft. Keep adding sticks until you reach your desired width.
2. Glue two sticks across the width of the raft perpendicular to the base; Place them toward the middle, keeping a space between them just wide enough to later support the twig mast.
3. When the glue is dried, turn the raft over and glue two sticks into place across the width again, near each end of the raft.
4. Let dry, turn over, and secure the twig mast in place, using a dollop of glue to hold. When dry, glue on a sail made from the colored paper.
5. Allow the glue to dry. When all is ship-shape, your child will be ready to set sail on a wild adventure in the bathtub.

SPEEDBOAT

scissors, milk carton, balloon

1. Using the scissors, cut the milk carton in half lengthwise. This should produce a boat-like shape.
2. Taking one of the halves, cut a round hole about half an inch in diameter in the middle of the flat bottom end.
3. Push the neck of the balloon through the hole, starting from the inside of the boat. Inflate the balloon, keeping the neck pinched close, and place the boat in the water. Releasing the neck will propel the boat through the water.

The Boy Who Cried Wolf

nce upon a time, a shepherd boy lived in a tiny village high in the tallest mountains. Every morning, he led the villagers' sheep up a steep, grassy hill to graze.

From the shady spot where he sat, he'd often look down at the ant-size villagers and wondered what it would be like to bake bread, give haircuts, or cobble shoes for a living, surrounded by other people instead of sheep. "It wouldn't be as boring as watching sheep," he muttered. "All sheep do is eat and sleep and say *Baa* all day. I'm so, sooooo bored!" Suddenly, he had idea.

"Wolf!" he cried loudly. "A wolf is chasing the sheep!"

The villagers immediately dropped what they were doing and hurried up the hill.

"I don't see a wolf," said the butcher, huffing and puffing from the steep climb.

"Our sheep are fine. What is going on here?" said the doctor, wiping the sweat from his brow.

"Oh! I just wanted some company!" said the shepherd boy.

"Don't cry 'wolf' when there's no wolf, or you'll be sorry," the

The Boy Who Cried Wolf

villagers scolded the shepherd boy. But the boy was laughing so hard tears ran down his cheeks.

The next day, from the shady spot where he sat, he looked down at the ant-size villagers again. And again he said, "All sheep do is eat and sleep and say *Baa* all day. I'm so, sooooo bored!" So again the boy yelled, "Wolf! Wolf! A wolf is chasing the sheep!"

Again, the villagers climbed the steep hill.

"I don't see a wolf," said the butcher, huffing and puffing even more than the day before.

"He did it again!" yelled the doctor.

"DON'T CRY 'WOLF' WHEN THERE IS NO WOLF, OR YOU'LL BE SORRY," they warned. But the shepherd boy just laughed, thrilled that he'd made his life more fun.

The next day it happened. From the top of the hill the boy saw a REAL wolf—furry, fierce, and drooling—sneaking from tree to tree, closer and closer.

"Wolf! Wolf!" the shepherd boy shouted in a panic. "WOLF! WOLF!"

The villagers heard him. But the butcher said, "He's doing it again!" And the doctor said, "I'm not running up that hill for nothing again." They thought the shepherd boy was trying to fool them like the two days before. This time they didn't come. And, just as the villagers had warned, the shepherd boy sure was sorry. With no one to help him, the shepherd boy lost all his sheep to the wolf.

The Boy Who Cried Wolf

Trees

Trees are one of the oldest living things on Earth. They are also the largest (even older and larger than the dinosaurs!). Whether they have a treehouse, can't wait to decorate the Christmas tree, or simply love the taste of maple syrup, children are a tree's most natural friends. Taking your child on a nature walk to identify different types of trees is a great way to introduce him or her to Mother Nature. Use these illustrations to identify the trees where you live, and to teach your child the names of his or her leafy friends.

HEMLOCK

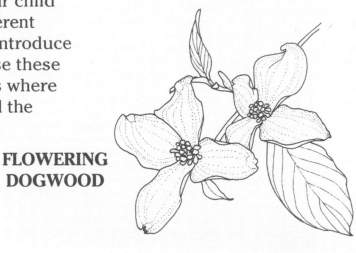

FLOWERING DOGWOOD

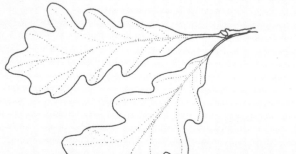

WHITE OAK

BALSAM FIR

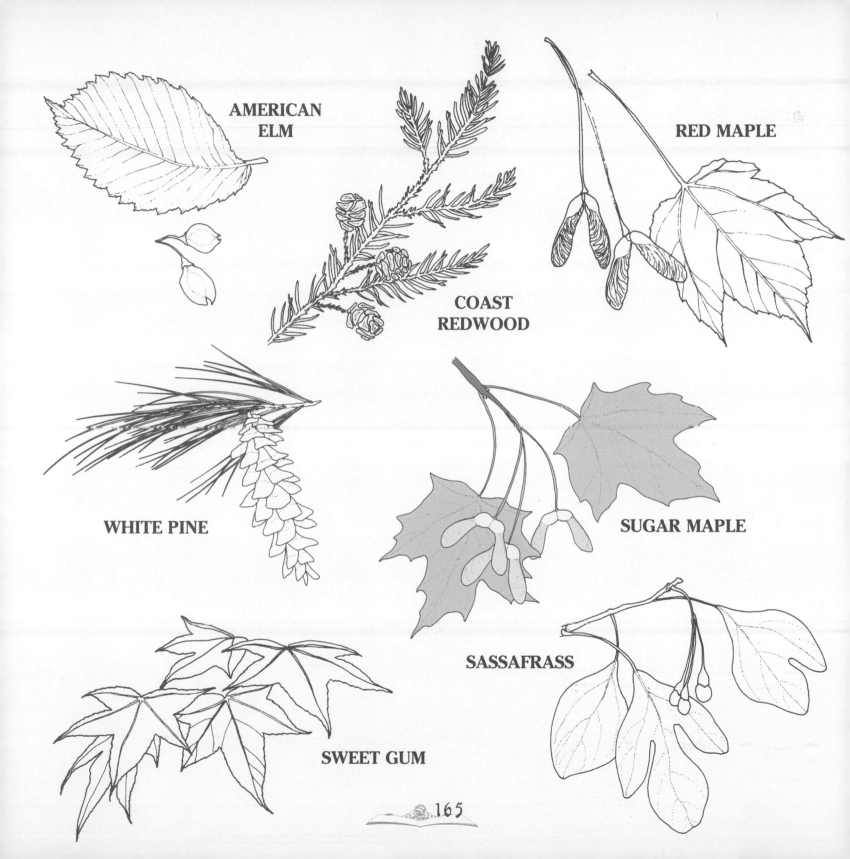

AMERICAN
ELM

COAST
REDWOOD

RED MAPLE

WHITE PINE

SUGAR MAPLE

SASSAFRASS

SWEET GUM

Swan swam over
Swim, swan,
Swan swam
Well swum

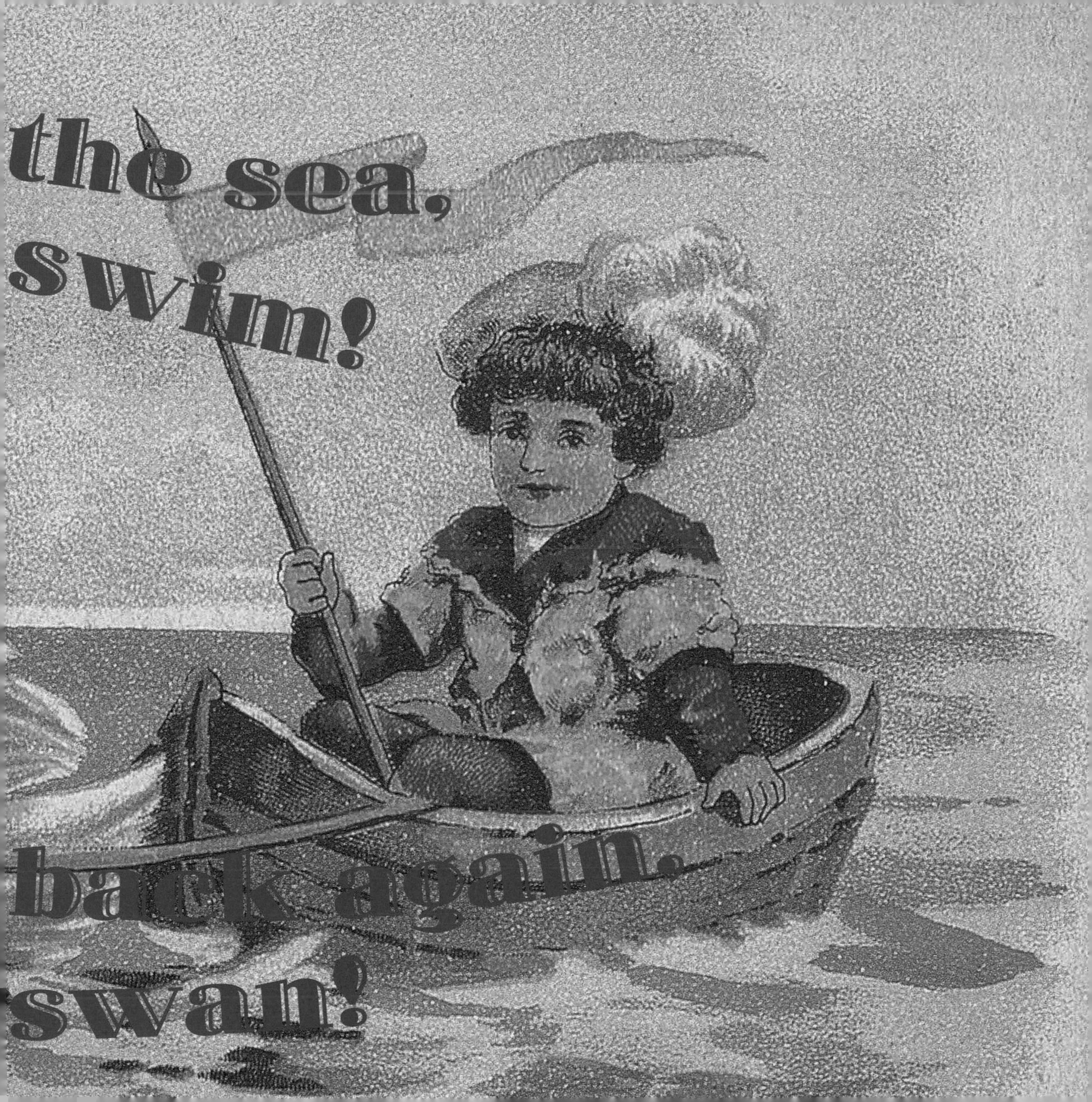
the sea,
swim!
back again.
swan!

Every survival kit
should include a
sense of humor
—Anonymous

Jack

Jack be nimble,

Jack be quick,

Jack jump over
the candle-stick.

I've Been Working on the Railroad

I've been work-ing on the rail - road all the live - long day.

I've been work-ing on the rail - road just to pass the time a - way.

Don't you hear the whis-tle blow - ing, rise up so ear - ly in the morn?

Don't you hear the cap-tain shout - ing, "Di - nah, blow your horn!"

I've Been Working on the Railroad

Di - nah won't you blow,   Di - nah won't you blow,

Di - nah won't you blow your   horn,   your   horn"

Di - nah won't you blow,   Di - nah won't you blow,

Di - nah won't   you blow   your   horn?

Some - one's in   the kitch - en with   Di - nah,

Some-one's in the kitch-en, I know, I know.

Some-one's in the kitch-en with Di - nah,

Strum-min' on the old ban - jo. Sing - ing

Fee, fie, fid-dle-e - i - o. Fee, fie, fid-dle-e - i - o - i - o.

Fee, fie, fid-dle-e - i - o, Strum-min'on the old ban - jo.

Aladdin and the Magic Lamp

nce upon a time, a poor tailor lived in a rich city in China. When he died, he left a wife, who had to spin cotton to earn a living, and a son named Aladdin.

One day, a strange man approached Aladdin in the street, pretending to be his uncle.

"I don't have an uncle," Aladdin said to the man, who was really an evil magician.

The magician insisted, and asked Aladdin to go for a walk with him. "If you come with me, I will make you a rich man," he said.

"Well, I'm not allowed to talk to strangers," said Aladdin. "But I'm sure my mother won't mind if I come home rich." And so they set off through the city, across fancy gardens and shady parks, and into the open country.

When they reached a narrow valley the magician said, "Mimbo! Limbo!" and *boom!* The earth cracked open before them.

"Wow!" Aladdin exclaimed, as he stared down into darkness.

"There's a door down there," the magician said. "I'm too big to fit through it, but you're not. Do as I say, and you'll be richer than

Aladdin and the Magic Lamp

the richest king."

"I will," Aladdin said, listening closely.

"Jump down," the magician instructed. "Then go through the door and walk until you reach a shelf. Take the lamp off the shelf and bring it to me. And don't touch anything besides the door and the lamp—or you'll die instantly!"

Then the magician took a ring from his pinkie finger and slid it onto Aladdin's middle finger. "This will protect you against evil."

Aladdin jumped into the hole and landed in soft dirt. He opened the door and hurried toward the shelf with the lamp. He stuffed it into a pocket and began to head back when something sparkly caught his eye.

He looked around and realized he was in an orchard. Fruits of the richest colors—red as rubies, green as emeralds, blue as sapphires—hung from the trees. Some were even as clear as diamonds! Forgetting his promise, Aladdin filled his pockets with the fruit, which he thought was made of glass, before returning to the magician, who peered down impatiently.

"Give me the lamp," the magician said.

Aladdin reached into his pockets, but there was so much fruit, he couldn't get to the lamp.

"Help me out first!" Aladdin said, extending his hand.

But the magician had no intention of letting Aladdin out at all.

Aladdin and the Magic Lamp

He just wanted the lamp. When Aladdin didn't obey him, he went into a rage. "Limbo! Mimbo!" he shouted, and *boom!* The earth slammed shut, leaving the boy alone in the darkness. Aladdin cried, "Help!" but his echo was the only answer. Very frightened, he began to cry, and rubbed his face to wipe away the tears.

"I AM THE SLAVE OF THE RING! WHAT IS YOUR WISH?" sounded a voice in the darkness.

Aladdin realized he'd accidentally rubbed the ring, his protection against evil.

"I want to be back home!" Aladdin said. And instantly, he was.

When he told his mother what had happened, she scolded him for going off with a stranger. "The fruit *is* pretty," she added, "but why would anyone want this dusty old lamp?" She began to rub off the dirt—and a genie appeared!

"WHAT IS YOUR WISH?" asked the genie, wiping dust from its eyes.

Too frightened to speak, Aladdin's mother handed the lamp to her son.

"Fetch us a feast," Aladdin said, for he was hungry and all they had in the cupboard were three stale rolls. Instantly the table was covered with silver platters of only the finest food and two silver cups filled with the sweetest tea in the world.

"Yummy!" Aladdin exclaimed, munching on a leg of lamb.

Aladdin and the Magic Lamp

"Chocolate truffles!" exclaimed his mother, popping one into her mouth.

They ate and ate until nothing was left. And the next morning, they sold the silver platters and cups for forty piles of gold, making them very rich.

One day, a few years later, the sultan (which means "king") announced that everyone should stay out of the streets while his daughter walked to her bath. But Aladdin, now a young man, ignored him. Instead, he hid in a doorway and glimpsed the princess as she passed with her maids. He was stunned by her beauty.

"I'm in love with the princess," Aladdin later told his mother. "I shall marry her!"

"Are you crazy?" said his mother. "We may be rich, but we are not royalty."

"I want you to go impress the sultan for me," Aladdin said confidently.

"Me!" cried his mother, though she knew it would be the proper thing to do. "But I have no valuable gift to present to him."

"The colorful fruit," Aladdin suggested.

"But they're only made of glass!" Aladdin's mother said.

"No," said Aladdin, who had taken them to a gem expert. "They are actually precious gems, and very valuable."

Aladdin and the Magic Lamp

So Aladdin's mother folded the fruit into fine cloth and set out for the palace.

"How exquisite!" the sultan cried when he saw the gems. "Even I have never seen such riches."

But although Aladdin's mother won the sultan's favor, he had already promised his daughter to an officer. "Here's what you must do," he said, admiring an emerald pear. "Have your son send me forty golden barrels of these gems delivered by forty costumed slaves, and he can marry my daughter." Aladdin's mother bowed and left, thinking all was lost.

When his mother broke the news to him, Aladdin immediately called the genie and repeated the sultan's request. The following day, a procession of forty costumed slaves marched through town, each carrying a golden barrel of diamonds, emeralds, rubies, and sapphires on his head. People watched with awe—but no one was more astonished than the sultan. "A wedding shall be planned at once," he pronounced.

Aladdin's mother, who had followed behind the slaves, was so excited she skipped all the way home. Aladdin, too, was overjoyed. He called the genie and wished for a marble palace fit for himself and the princess—and his mother. He also asked for a white horse and forty thousand pieces of gold. As he rode to the palace, he tossed gold into the streets, winning the affection of

Aladdin and the Magic Lamp

the people. And when the princess met Aladdin, she fell in love at once and the couple lived happily for years.

Then one day, the magician, who never dreamt Aladdin could have escaped from the cave, looked into his crystal ball and saw Aladdin rich and happy. He left his home in Africa and set off for China in a rage.

When he reached the palace, he was told Aladdin was out hunting.

"Then I must work fast," he said to himself, whipping up five shiny copper lamps. "Trade old lamps for new lamps!" he cried, setting up shop beneath the princess's window.

Hearing the magician's cry, the princess grabbed Aladdin's old lamp—not knowing about the genie—and hurried outside. "Here," she said, thinking the stranger must be stupid to take an old lamp for a new one.

The magician gave the princess a new lamp, hurried into the forest, and rubbed the old one. When the genie appeared, the magician ordered him to take Aladdin's palace and the princess to Africa. Immediately, the palace and the princess disappeared magically.

Deeply grieved by the disappearance of his daughter, the sultan sent for Aladdin. "If you don't find my daughter in forty days, I'll chop off your head," he told his son-in-law.

Aladdin and the Magic Lamp

Feeling more sad than afraid, Aladdin searched all over China for his wife and palace but had no luck. Frustrated, he put his head in his hands.

"I AM THE SLAVE OF THE RING! WHAT IS YOUR WISH?"

Aladdin looked up, hopeful.

"I want my wife and palace back," Aladdin cried, realizing he had, again, accidentally rubbed the ring.

"Only the genie of the lamp can grant you that," said the slave of the ring.

"The genie's in the palace," Aladdin said. "So take me there."

Instantly he found himself outside his palace, which was now in a strange land.

"Aladdin!" cried the princess, who had been weeping at her window.

Aladdin raced to embrace her. She told him that she had given away the lamp—and immediately Aladdin knew the magician was behind it.

"I must have that lamp," Aladdin said.

"But the magician never lets it out of

Aladdin and the Magic Lamp

his sight," replied the princess, who in her captivity had learned the habits of the wicked man.

She and Aladdin came up with a plan.

That night, the princess asked the magician to dine with her. He gladly accepted and took a sip of the wine she offered him, which Aladdin had mixed with a poisonous powder. Instantly, the magician fell to the floor, dead.

Aladdin grabbed the lamp and, in no time at all, he, the princess, and the palace were back in China where they belonged. After the sultan died, they came to rule the kingdom and lived happily ever after.

Balloon Fun

Children love balloons! The first activity is educational, and a great introduction to experimenting and science. The suggestions that follow are a reminder of all the fun and simple things you can do with balloons. *(Remember that balloons present a choking hazard and supervise young children accordingly.)*

GAS BALLOON

balloon, empty bottle with a small neck, funnel, vinegar, baking soda

1. Placing the funnel into the mouth of the bottle, help your child put two teaspoons of baking soda into the bottle.
2. Pour $1/3$ cup of vinegar into the balloon using the funnel.
3. Stretch the neck of the balloon over the mouth of the bottle, pulling it on securely. You may want to hold onto the neck for support, since the reaction can sometimes be quite strong.
4. Hold the balloon upright to allow the vinegar to start mixing with the baking soda. The mixture should begin fizzing, expanding the balloon at an enormous rate.
5. You can explain to your child that gas is "hidden" in the baking soda. The gas that inflates the balloon is caused by the reaction between the vinegar, which is high in acetic acid, and the baking soda (also called sodium bicarbonate).

MORE BALLOON FUN

1. Blow a balloon up really big and then let it go. (Make sure you have enough room.)
2. Make wonderful noises by blowing up a balloon and releasing the air slowly while stretching the end of the balloon neck.
3. Rub an inflated balloon against a wooly sweater and then stick it to your hair.
4. Fill a small balloon with water for the bath or outdoors. Younger children love the feel of them in their hands.
5. Impress someone with this "magic" trick. Tape a small piece of scotch tape to an inflated balloon. If you stick a pin through the taped area, the balloon will not pop.

Knock knock!

Will you remember
me tomorrow?
Will you remember
me the next day?
Will you remember
me the next next day?

Knock Knock

Who's there?

Hey! You've forgotten
me already!

Knock Knock

Who's there?

Olive.

Olive who?

Olive you, sweetie!

Knock Knock

Who's there?

Lettuce.

Lettuce who?

Lettuce in! Gotta use
the bathroom!

Knock Knock

Who's there?

Cockadoodle.

Cockadoodle who?

Cockadoodle WHO? No,
it's cockadoodle DOO!

Knock Knock

Who's there?

Harry.

Harry who?

Harry up and
open the door!

Knock Knock

Who's there?

Betty.

Betty who?

Betty-bye! Time
to go to bed!

Knock Knock

Who's there?

Heaven.

Heaven who?

Heaven you heard
enough knock knock
jokes yet?

Who's there?

Snowy Day Fun

As early winter's tiny snowflakes begin to drift past your window, tell your children that it's good luck to catch snowflakes on their tongues—it's the season's first snow activity, and it just might keep them entertained for a while. But as the snow begins to accumulate, there is more fun to be had, and outdoor playtime is a requisite. Don't forget snowball fights!

SNOW FAMILY
at least 4 inches of fresh snow, sticks, buttons

1. Start by making a snowball, and then rolling it around in the snow, changing directions every so often to make it nice and round. Keep rolling the ball in fresh snow until it's as large as you want it.
2. Make three snowballs: a large base, a medium body, a small head. Pile them on top of one another.
3. Use sticks for arms and buttons for eyes, nose, and mouth. Instead of making just one snowman, make an entire snow family modeled after your own. Dress up each snowperson with a personal belonging of each family member!

SNOW ANGELS
snow

1. Have your little angel lay on a fresh patch of snow.
3. He or she should go through the motion of "jumping jacks," but while laying on the ground.
3. Help your child get up carefully so as not to disturb the angel impression.

COLORED SNOW
snow, food coloring, spray bottle

1. Mix some food coloring in water, and then pour it into spray bottles.
2. Spray the colorful mixture onto the snow, drawing pictures or writing messages that will last . . . until the next snowfall.

Whether the

Whether the weather be cold
or whether the weather be hot.
We'll weather the weather
whatever the weather
whether we like it or not.

or whether the

A Rainbow of Colors

Children love colors. Ask any young child his or her favorite color and he or she will give you a list of several colors. Painting would not be much fun if there was only black paint! Let your child thrill in the magic of colors with the following face and finger painting activities. Then explore the most wonderful colorful thing of all, a rainbow, by creating a few of your own.

MAKE A RAINBOW
deep baking pan, water, small mirror, flashlight, piece of white paper

1. Pour water in the baking pan.
2. Angle the mirror against the side of the pan so that a part of the mirror is not submerged in the water.
3. Shine the flashlight on the submerged part of the mirror.
4. While holding the light steady with one hand, hold the paper behind and above the light with the other. Your rainbow will be projected onto the paper. Trade places with your child and take turns making the rainbows.

FACE PAINTS
cornstarch, water, cold cream, food coloring, 6 small cups or a muffin tin, popsicle stick, paintbrush

1. Add 1 teaspoon cornstarch, $1/2$ teaspoon water, $1/3$ teaspoon cold cream, and a few drops of food coloring to each cup. Use a different color in each cup.
2. Stir with popsicle stick to mix color evenly. Hand your child the paintbrush, sit down, and let your child make a colorful Dad!

FINGER PAINTS
shaving cream, food coloring

1. Add different colors to mounds of shaving cream. That's it! The shaving

cream method is best to try out in the bathtub, where kids can make as much of a colorful mess painting on bathroom walls and each other as they want.

2. Turn on the water and clean up everything, including your children.

RAINBOW IN BOTTLES

6 clear, empty bottles; red, blue, and yellow food coloring

1. Fill the bottles with water. Add food coloring to each bottle, using each color for two bottles. Your child will love to watch as the dyes fall to the bottom, spreading out and coloring everything their wake. Explain to your child that red, blue, and yellow are primary colors.

2. When the colors have sufficiently settled, teach your child about secondary colors and color combinations. Add red to one blue bottle to make purple, yellow to a red bottle to make orange, blue to a yellow bottle to make green.

3. Let your child gently shake the bottles to finish coloring the water, and then sit the bottles in a place where the sun will shine through them.

FUN FACTS:
- A rainbow is created by sunlight passing through water droplets in the atmosphere after rain.
- Sunlight passing through water is broken up into the spectrum of colors to create the seven colors in a rainbow.
- The colors of the rainbow are always in the exact same order. The colors from the widest outside arch to the smallest inside arch closest to the horizon are red, orange, yellow, green, blue, indigo, and violet.

Rain

Rain, rain, go away,

Come again another day;

Little Johnny wants to play.

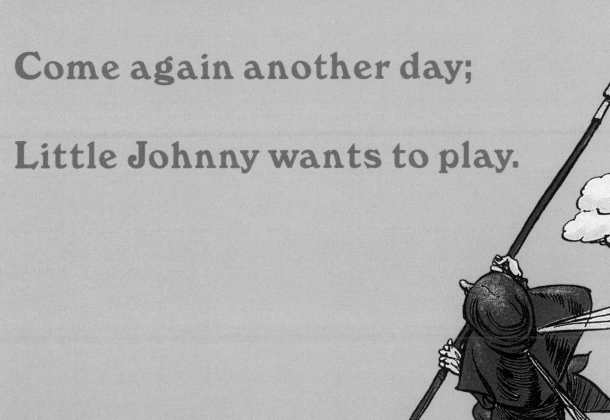

The Shoemaker and the Elves

Once upon a time there lived a very poor shoemaker. Though he made the best shoes in town, very few of his customers had enough money to pay him for them.

"Pay what you can afford," he would say, accepting such gifts as flowers or a chicken. "No one should have to go barefoot."

"You're a good man," his wife often said, as their customers walked away in shiny new shoes.

As time went on, the shoemaker became poorer and poorer until all he had left was enough leather for one pair of shoes. That evening he cut the leather and left it on his worktable. "I'll finish them in the morning," he said, turning out the light.

The next morning, the shoemaker and his wife woke to a great surprise! For there on the worktable was a finished pair of shoes. After closely examining the shoes, the shoemaker shook his head with wonder. "Every stitch is perfect!" he said. "Who could have done this?"

Just then, a richly dressed man entered the shop and tried the shoes on. "What a perfect fit!" he said, and paid the shoemaker

The Shoemaker and the Elves

enough money to buy leather for two more pairs of shoes.

That evening, the shoemaker cut the leather and planned to work on the shoes in the morning. But by morning, two finished pairs of shoes sat on the worktable.

This time, a richly dressed woman bought both pairs and gave the shoemaker so much money, he was able to buy enough leather for four pairs of shoes. Again, he cut the leather in the evening, and the shoes were finished by morning—this time, earning him enough money to buy leather for ten pairs of shoes!

After several weeks of this, the very poor shoemaker had become a very rich shoemaker. On the night before Christmas, after the leather had been cut, the shoemaker said to his wife, "Let's stay up tonight and see who's been making the shoes."

"Good idea!" said his wife. "We can light a lantern and hide behind the coatrack."

As the clock struck midnight, they watched in awe as ten tiny, naked elves marched into the shop and gathered round the worktable. Quickly and quietly, with deep concentration, they stitched and pierced and hammered until thirty perfect pairs of shoes sat lined up in a row. Then, quick as a wink, they marched out of the shop.

"Those precious elves have made us rich!" said the shoemaker.

"They must be freezing!" said his wife. "I'm going to make ten

The Shoemaker and the Elves

tiny sets of clothes, using the best threads and patterns."

"And I'm going to make ten tiny pairs of shoes," said the shoemaker. "It's the least we can do to say thank you."

The next morning, the shoemaker and his wife got right to work. It didn't take long to make such tiny sizes, and they finished well before suppertime. That night, in place of leather, they laid out ten tiny shirts, ten tiny pairs of overalls, ten tiny snowsuits, ten tiny hats, ten tiny pairs of mittens, and ten tiny pairs of shoes. Then they lit the lantern and hid behind the coatrack.

At midnight, the shoemaker and his wife watched the ten tiny, naked elves march into the shop and gasp in delight! They loved the tiny outfits and giggled as they dressed. Then, in high, tinkling voices, they sang a thank-you song and danced a silly jig. At the first light of day, they skipped straight out the door—never to be seen again.

From that day on, the shoemaker's business did better than ever—though he still accepted yo-yo's, pinecones, and handkerchiefs when a customer couldn't afford to pay. Because, he and his wife agreed, no one should have to go barefoot.

Bye, baby bunting,

Father's gone a-hunting,

Mother's gone a-milking,

Sister's gone a-silking,

And brother's gone to buy a skin

To wrap the baby bunting in.

Bye, Baby Bunting

Where Did You Come From, Baby Dear?

by George MacDonald

Where did you come from, baby dear?
Out of the everywhere into here.

Where did you get your eyes so blue?
Out of the sky as I came through.

What makes the light in them sparkle and spin?
Some of the starry spikes left in.

Where did you get that little tear?
I found it waiting when I got here.

What makes your forehead so smooth and high?
A soft hand stroked it as I went by.

What makes your cheek like a warm white rose?
I saw something better than anyone knows.

Whence that three-cornered smile of bliss?
Three angels gave me at once a kiss.

Where did you get this pearly ear?
God spoke, and it came out to hear.

Where did you get those arms and hands?
Love made itself into hooks and bands.

Feet, whence did you come, you darling things?
From the same box as the cherubs' wings.

How did they all just come to be you?
God thought about me, and so I grew.

But how did you come to us, you dear?
God thought about you, and so I am here.

Is there anything sweeter than this?

—Anonymous

Starry Skies

Staring up at the night sky on a warm summer night is one of the enduring pleasures of life. Philosophers, poets, and scientists alike have marveled at the cosmos, musing about its beauty and origin. Maybe you can't unravel the mysteries of the universe for your children, but you can tell them the stories of the stars and the constellations, those silent sentinels who keep us company through the night, and have for centuries held deep meaning for different peoples of the world. A telescope is not necessary to find the following constellations —all that's needed is a beautiful, clear night, and curious, young eyes and ears.

Hercules was a son of Zeus, and a favorite among the gods. He was forced to perform twelve impossible acts as punishment for killing his wife and children while ill with a temporary fit of insanity. By completing these tasks, he proved himself to be a *hero* —perhaps the greatest of Greek heroes—a word that is derived from his name.

Leo was a great lion whom Hercules was sent to kill in his first "impossible act." No weapon was able to pierce the lion's skin, and so Hercules, in order to kill him, trapped him inside a cave, and thrust his fist deep into Leo's throat. Once Hercules had taken the dead lion to show the king that he had succeeded, he used the hide as a protective shield to aid him in the rest of his twelve tasks.

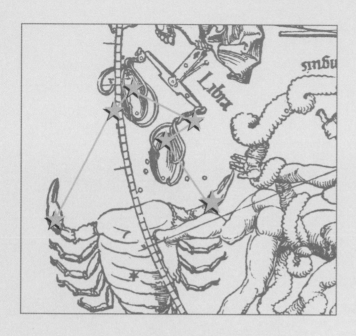

Libra is one of the signs of the zodiac, and has come to represent balance and justice. The constellation forms the "Scales of Justice" of Julius Caesar. Libra, as a constellation, is also part of Scorpius, and forms the claws of this great scorpion.

Pegasus was a winged horse that Zeus used to carry his thunderbolts and later placed among the stars. He was both a magical and playful creature, and his image today is recognized as a symbol of poetry.

216

Starry Skies

Sagittarius sits right in the heart of the Milky Way. Half man, half horse, this archer—according to mythology—was set in the skies to help navigators at sea find their way. He is also one of the signs of the zodiac.

Ursa Major and **Ursa Minor** are more commonly referred to as the Big Dipper and the Little Dipper, though if you look beyond this common arrangement of stars, you see that they are, in fact, both *bears*. Originally the mistress and son of Zeus (Callisto and Arcas), he changed them into animals to protect them from Hera, his wife, who was trying to kill them, and carried them into the sky by their long tails (these bears have longer tails than present-day bears, and these tails make up the handles of the big and little dippers). Hera convinced Poseidon (the sea god) not to let them bathe in the sea, and so they can be seen hovering just above the horizon, making them always visible in the night sky.

Twinkle, Twinkle, Little Star

by Jane Taylor

Twinkle, twinkle, little star,
How I wonder what you are!
Up above the world so high,
Like a diamond in the sky.

When the blazing sun is gone,
When he nothing shines upon,
Then you show your little light,
Twinkle, twinkle all the night.

Then the traveler in the dark,
Thanks you for your tiny spark,
He could not see which way to go
If you did not twinkle so.

In the dark blue sky you keep,
And often through my curtains peep,
For you never shut your eye,
'Til the sun is in the sky.

As your bright and tiny spark
Lights the travelaer in the dark—
Though I know not what you are,
Twinkle, twinkle, little star.

Sleep, Baby, Sleep

Sleep, ba - by, sleep, Your fa - ther's watch-ing his

sheep, Your moth - er shakes ___ the

dream - land tree, A lit - tle dream ___ falls

down for thee, Sleep, ba - by, sleep.

Hush Little Baby

Anonymous

Hush little baby, don't say a word,
Papa's going to buy you a mockingbird.

If that mockingbird won't sing,
Papa's going to buy you a diamond ring.

If that diamond ring turns brass,
Papa's going to buy you a looking glass.

If that looking glass gets broke,
Papa's going to buy you a billy goat.

If that billy goat won't pull,
Papa's going to buy you a cart and bull.

If that cart and bull fall down,
You'll still be the sweetest little baby in town.

Make the most
of every day
For time does
not stand still.
One day this hand
will wave good-bye
While crossing
life's brave hill.

—Anonymous